Supervising and Managing People

"*People ask you for criticism, but they only want praise.*"

—W. Somerset Maugham

Supervising and Managing People

McGraw-Hill

New York   San Francisco   Washington, D.C.   Auckland   Bogotá
Caracas   Lisbon   London   Madrid   Mexico City   Milan
Montreal   New Delhi   San Juan   Singapore   Sydney   Tokyo   Toronto

Other *First Books for Business* include:

Budgeting and Finance

Business Presentations and Public Speaking

Negotiating

Sales and Marketing

This book is printed on acid-free paper.

Library of Congress Cataloging-in-Publication Data

Supervising & managing people.
        p.   cm.—(First books for business)
   Includes bibliographical references and index.
   ISBN 0-07-001569-4
   1. Supervision of employees. 2. Personnel management. I. Title:
  Supervising and managing people II. Series.
  HF5549.12.S855   1996
  658.3'02—dc20   96-7830
                                         CIP

5 6 7 8 9 0 DOW/DOW 9 0 1 0

ISBN 0-07-001569-4

Developed for McGraw-Hill by Affinity Communications Corp., 144 N. Robertson Blvd., Suite 103, Los Angeles, CA 90048

Conceptual Development by Mari Florence Editorial and Frank Loose Design

Designer:	Frank Loose Design
Developmental Editor:	Mari Florence
Production Editor:	Nancy McKinley
Technical Consultant:	Robert Moskowitz

McGraw-Hill books are available at special quantity discounts to use as premiums and sales promotions, or for use in corporate training programs. For more information, please write to the Director of Special Sales, McGraw-Hill, 11 West 19th Street, New York, NY 10011. Or contact your local bookstore.

Table of Contents

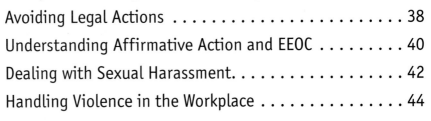

Chapter 8: Effective Discipline

Chapter 9: Effective Leadership

Appendix

How to Use This Book

We created *First Books for Business* to provide answers to your most pressing questions. In developing this series, we brought together an expert panel of top-notch businesspeople who shared with us their flair for success.

By taking the best of this wealth of information and presenting it in 50 colorful two-page chapters, you'll be able to easily understand the most important elements of the art of doing business. Each chapter features special information elements where you can find help to gain a deeper understanding of the discussed topic. Here's how to best use this book:

1 *Inside Info*
Check out this feature to go behind the scenes and learn what the real pros already know!

2 *Words to Live By*
Read these inspirational, witty, or tongue-in-cheek observations that you can use to motivate yourself—or just for fun.

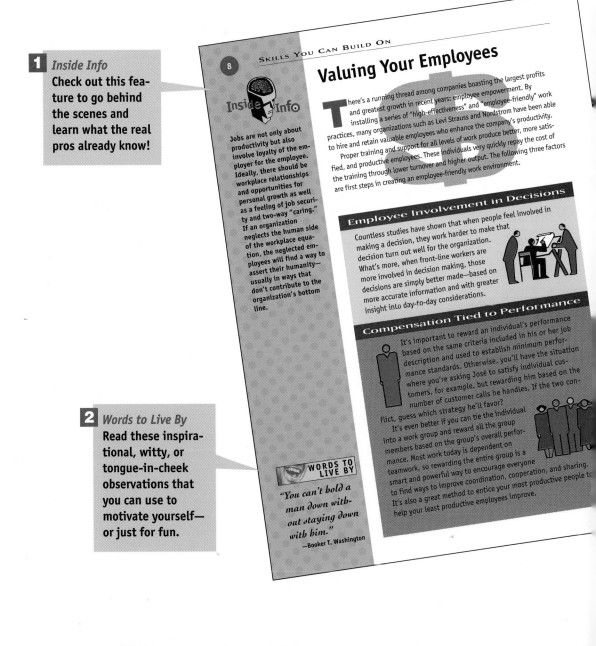

8   SKILLS YOU CAN BUILD ON

Valuing Your Employees

There's a running thread among companies boasting the largest profits and greatest growth in recent years: employee empowerment. By installing a series of "high-effectiveness" and "employee-friendly" work practices, many organizations such as Levi Strauss and Nordstrom have been able to hire and retain valuable employees who enhance the company's productivity.

Proper training and support for all levels of work produce better, more satisfied, and productive employees. These individuals very quickly repay the cost of the training through lower turnover and higher output. The following three factors are first steps in creating an employee-friendly work environment.

Employee Involvement in Decisions

Countless studies have shown that when people feel involved in making a decision, they work harder to make that decision turn out well for the organization. What's more, when front-line workers are more involved in decision making, those decisions are simply better made—based on more accurate information and with greater insight into day-to-day considerations.

Compensation Tied to Performance

It's important to reward an individual's performance based on the same criteria included in his or her job description and used to establish minimum performance standards. Otherwise, you'll have the situation where you're asking José to satisfy individual customers, for example, but rewarding him based on the number of customer calls he handles. If the two conflict, guess which strategy he'll favor?

It's even better if you can tie the individual into a work group and reward all the group members based on the group's overall performance. Most work today is dependent on teamwork, so rewarding the entire group is a smart and powerful way to encourage everyone to find ways to improve coordination, cooperation, and sharing. It's also a great method to entice your most productive people to help your least productive employees improve.

Inside Info

Jobs are not only about productivity but also involve loyalty of the employer for the employee. Ideally, there should be workplace relationships and opportunities for personal growth as well as a feeling of job security and two-way "caring." If an organization neglects the human side of the workplace equation, the neglected employees will find a way to assert their humanity—usually in ways that don't contribute to the organization's bottom line.

WORDS TO LIVE BY

"You can't hold a man down without staying down with him."
—Booker T. Washington

Making Delegation Work

For many supervisors and managers, it often seems quicker and easier to do the job yourself than to delegate it to one of your team members. To deal with these feelings, start by delegating projects such as monthly reports—which have to be done again and again. This way, your time investment is well spent by educating an individual who can take over this project and take it off your plate.

3 Skill Builders
Practice—and master—a new skill that will help you better understand and apply the information you've learned in this book.

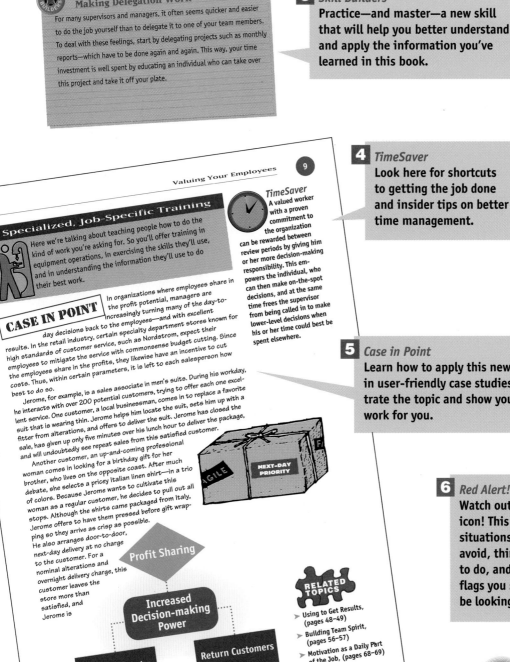

Specialized, Job-Specific Training

Here we're talking about teaching people how to do the kind of work you're asking for. So you'll offer training in equipment operations, in exercising the skills they'll use, and in understanding the information they'll use to do their best work.

CASE IN POINT

In organizations where employees share in the profit potential, managers are increasingly turning many of the day-to-day decisions back to the employees—and with excellent results. In the retail industry, certain specialty department stores known for high standards of customer service, such as Nordstrom, expect their employees to mitigate the service with commonsense budget cutting. Since the employees share in the profits, they likewise have an incentive to cut costs. Thus, within certain parameters, it is left to each salesperson how best to do so.

Jerome, for example, is a sales associate in men's suits. During his workday, he interacts with over 200 potential customers, trying to offer each one excellent service. One customer, a local businessman, comes in to replace a favorite suit that is wearing thin. Jerome helps him locate the suit, sets him up with a fitter from alterations, and offers to deliver the suit. Jerome has closed the sale, has given up only five minutes over his lunch hour to deliver the package, and will undoubtedly see repeat sales from this satisfied customer.

Another customer, an up-and-coming professional woman comes in looking for a birthday gift for her brother, who lives on the opposite coast. After much debate, she selects a pricey Italian linen shirt—in a trio of colors. Because Jerome wants to cultivate this woman as a regular customer, he decides to pull out all stops. Although the shirts came packaged from Italy, Jerome offers to have them pressed before gift wrapping so they arrive as crisp as possible. He also arranges door-to-door, next-day delivery at no charge to the customer. For a nominal alterations and overnight delivery charge, this customer leaves the store more than satisfied, and Jerome is

TimeSaver
A valued worker with a proven commitment to the organization can be rewarded between review periods by giving him or her more decision-making responsibility. This empowers the individual, who can then make on-the-spot decisions, and at the same time frees the supervisor from being called in to make lower-level decisions when his or her time could best be spent elsewhere.

4 TimeSaver
Look here for shortcuts to getting the job done and insider tips on better time management.

5 Case in Point
Learn how to apply this new information in user-friendly case studies that illustrate the topic and show you how it can work for you.

Profit Sharing

Increased Decision-making Power

Excellent Service

Return Customers

NEXT-DAY PRIORITY

RELATED TOPICS

▶ Using to Get Results, (pages 48–49)
▶ Building Team Spirit, (pages 56–57)
▶ Motivation as a Daily Part of the Job, (pages 68–69)

6 Red Alert!
Watch out for this icon! This tells you situations to avoid, things *not* to do, and red flags you should be looking for.

RED ALERT! Be careful to give your delegate enough leeway to do things his or her own way. The extra freedom you permit will translate into additional motivation to do a top-quality job. You'll also help your delegate gain more on-the-job experience and confidence.

7 Related Topics
See other pages to learn more new and challenging ways of doing business.

Establishing Your Credibility

Each of these individuals appears professional on first impression. Yet good supervision and management depends on more than your skills and personality. It requires a degree of credibility with those you hope to lead. In rare cases, certain people seem to have a natural gift for instantly establishing their credibility in others' eyes—whether the impression is valid or not. However, most individuals must work hard to build and maintain credibility from the very first moment they meet people.

There are several guidelines to help speed the growth and development of your credibility in new situations:

WORDS TO LIVE BY

"Truth for authority, not authority for truth."

—Lucretia Mott

Be SURE of Yourself

Once you have established your credibility, a normal amount of mistakes won't reduce it. But when you're first trying to build your level of credibility, it's important to be a little more sure of yourself in the early stages of your new supervisory or managerial situation. Before you speak or act, take the time to check your facts more than once, go over your reasoning or your computations again, and/or run your ideas past someone you know and respect to gauge his or her reaction.

Say LESS instead of MORE

A curious phenomenon is that people often imbue silences with much more than is really there. If you refrain from meaningless chatter, people will generally assume that your silences conceal intelligence and wisdom. Thus, the less you say, the more credence people will grant to the few things you *do* say.

Don't become DEFENSIVE

You can easily destroy the credibility you've worked so hard to attain by displaying a negative, defensive attitude. This has the effect of giving your words and deeds the accompanying message: "You won't give this any more credibility than you've given me in the past."

Such a message puts people off. It irritates them, makes them defensive, and tends to interfere with the normal process of developing credibility. Even if you feel slightly defensive, try not to let anyone sense it in you.

SKILL BUILDERS — Listening

Building credibility is much like building dignity: You can't do it all in a day, and the harder you try, the more you spin your wheels. To boost your credibility, try gathering feedback from your colleagues about projects and judgments in which their expertise would be helpful. By asking, and then listening to their responses, you're less inclined to make hasty—and often embarrassing—decisions, and you can begin to build solid, reciprocal relationships within your company.

RELATED TOPICS

➤ Giving Effective Feedback, (pages 46–47)

➤ Resolving Conflicts Effectively, (pages 88–89)

Inside Info

Your First Weeks at a New Job

Whether you're newly promoted to your supervisory responsibilities or are bringing years of experience to a new organization, the first few weeks offer a unique opportunity and a challenge to establish yourself.

What could happen during these first few weeks? Expect almost anything—from the intrigue of office politics to an occasional embarrassing moment.

During the first days and weeks on the job, there will be a lot of specialized information to learn. Trying to write it all down can be time-consuming and tedious, but well worth it. Carry a pocket notebook and pencil or pen to use unobtrusively for jotting down critically important information, such as:

- names of key people with whom you'll be working

- first assignments and their deadlines

- policies and procedures you're expected to support

Make dozens, or even hundreds, of "first impressions" on subordinates, colleagues, and superiors in the organization.

Establish a lasting tone on such important matters as your on-the-job relationships, your competence, your approachability, your suitability for achievement and advancement, and much, much more.

Cosmocom, Inc.

555 Columbia Way
Columbia Park, CA 93015
310-555-0000

Janice Fernandez
Vice President, Marketing

Monday, March 22

8 START NEW JOB!   informational lunch
   new boss—   meeting w/account
9   Janice Fernandez   group
          ☺   sit in on status mtg. 3

10

11 meet w/support staff   5

12

Tuesday, March 23

                                  follow up
                                  w/Janice
8
   phone call to Technos   2:30 teleconference   2
                            w/cosmocom suppliers 3
                            software upgrade
                                 seminar   4
                                                  5

Wednesday, March 24

                    1:30 tour manufacturing
                         plant w/Janice   1
8
9 budget meeting   2

10   clean earthquake dust   3
                          from desk...   4
11 Jonny—
    6:30 Hayesfield
12   SOFTBALL TONIGHT!   5

Asking Questions

Every new position "requires learning the ropes," and it's not a bad reflection on your experience to regularly ask, "How is this done here?" until you've mainstreamed into the company. By expressing a willingness to learn "their way," you will better establish a rapport with your colleagues and superiors, and they'll likely be better disposed toward you—making your transition much smoother.

RED ALERT!

Be prepared to play defense in the intricate game of office politics. In your first few days, you'll be invited and/or excluded by certain camps, cliques, and cadres within the organization—often without your conscious understanding of the situation. How you choose to align yourself with or against them can have important ramifications on how well you can perform in your new assignment.

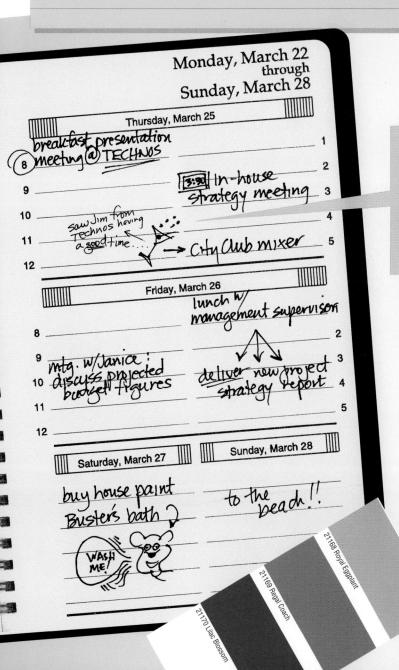

> **Monday, March 22**
> through
> **Sunday, March 28**
>
> **Thursday, March 25**
>
> breakfast presentation
> (8) meeting @ TECHNOS   1
> 2
> 3:30 In-house
> strategy meeting   3
> 9
> 10   saw Jim from Technos having   4
> 11   a good time.... → City Club mixer   5
> 12
>
> **Friday, March 26**
>
> lunch w/ management supervisor
> 8   2
> 9   mtg. w/Janice: discuss projected budget figures   3
> 10   deliver new project strategy report   4
> 11   5
> 12
>
> **Saturday, March 27**   **Sunday, March 28**
>
> buy house paint
> Buster's bath?   to the beach!!
> WASH ME!

Face at least one embarrassing moment. How you handle it will form the basis on which others treat you—possibly for the rest of the time you're with the organization.

21168 Royal Eggplant

21169 Regal Coach

21170 Lilac Blossom

RELATED TOPICS

> ▶ **Running Better Meetings,** (pages 22–23)
> ▶ **Setting Goals,** (pages 26–27)

Inside Info

At best, a promotion or new job is a challenge. And although dealing with unhappy coworkers can be complicated, remember these vital points: Each of you were chosen for employment for the qualities you could bring to the company. For each and every one of you, these jobs mean your livelihood. Although feelings may get hurt when professional and friendly relationships overlap, you shouldn't forget the basic reason you're all there—to work.

Maintaining On-the-Job Relationships

Today, supervisors and managers are urged to follow new model, a more compassionate, collaborative approach to leadership based on a philosophy of individual empowerment and team effort—a far cry from the Dickensian model of cold, miserly authority figures.

This modern approach to supervision and management has many important advantages. It engages more of the workers' intelligence, creativity, motivation, and loyalty and tends to reduce absenteeism and turnover, while increasing productivity and problem solving.

But it also creates a new difficulty for supervisors and managers: the need to understand and act on the inevitable and necessary distinctions that remain between those we supervise and manage—regardless of how well we apply modern ideas of "empowerment"—and our actual friends.

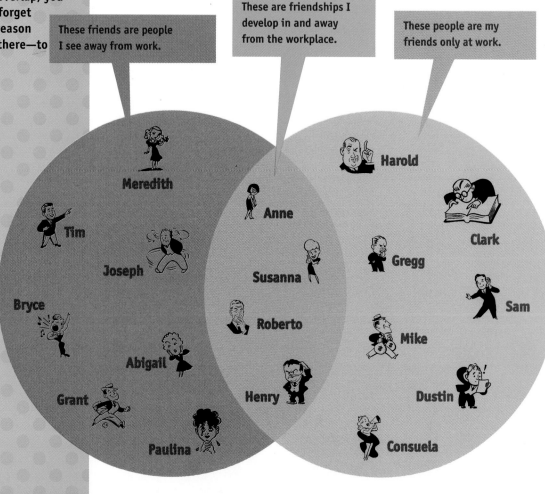

 Janice Chen works in the front office of a small company that manufactures circuit boards for home electronics systems. Recently, her hard work was rewarded when she was made office manager of the eight-person division and, as part of her new duties, was asked to get to the bottom of the high long-distance telephone bills. Of course, Janice knew who was largely responsible for placing them. Although most employees weren't using their work phones for personal calls, Diana in Accounts Payable had been using the phone constantly to call her daughter, who was attending college several hundred miles away.

The dilemma? As the office manager, Janice was required to report this to her employer. But, if she did, she realized the animosity that would result between "management" versus "employees."

To make the best of an uncomfortable situation, Janice chose to confront Diana and let her know that their employer was aware of the excessive phone charges and was trying to get to the bottom of it. Fortunately for Janice, Diana was responsive to this approach, and the two of them were able to work out the situation without creating an unpleasant working environment.

If you have been promoted to an authority position over colleagues you consider friends, there may be tension when you begin to supervise the people who were previously your equals. Such a reaction is normal. Behave equitably and kindly, and everyone should eventually adjust to the transition. Try to avoid becoming defensive and overreacting, since your actions could exacerbate the situation and make it more difficult to effectively supervise.

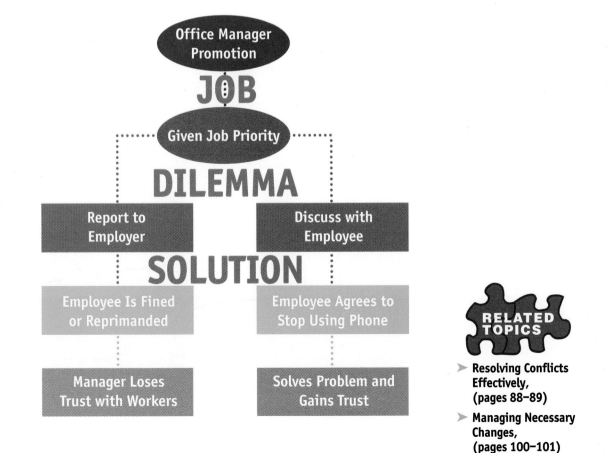

RELATED TOPICS

➤ Resolving Conflicts Effectively, (pages 88–89)

➤ Managing Necessary Changes, (pages 100–101)

Jobs are not only about productivity but also involve loyalty of the employer for the employee. Ideally, there should be workplace relationships and opportunities for personal growth as well as a feeling of job security and two-way "caring." If an organization neglects the human side of the workplace equation, the neglected employees will find a way to assert their humanity—usually in ways that don't contribute to the organization's bottom line.

"You can't hold a man down without staying down with him."
—Booker T. Washington

Valuing Your Employees

There's a running thread among companies boasting the largest profits and greatest growth in recent years: employee empowerment. By installing a series of "high-effectiveness" and "employee-friendly" work practices, many organizations such as Levi Strauss and Nordstrom have been able to hire and retain valuable employees who enhance the company's productivity.

Proper training and support for all levels of work produce better, more satisfied, and productive employees. These individuals very quickly repay the cost of the training through lower turnover and higher output. The following three factors are first steps in creating an employee-friendly work environment.

Employee Involvement in Decisions

Countless studies have shown that when people feel involved in making a decision, they work harder to make that decision turn out well for the organization. What's more, when front-line workers are more involved in decision making, those decisions are simply better made—based on more accurate information and with greater insight into day-to-day considerations.

Compensation Tied to Performance

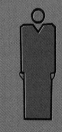 It's important to reward an individual's performance based on the same criteria included in his or her job description and used to establish minimum performance standards. Otherwise, you'll have the situation where you're asking José to satisfy individual customers, for example, but rewarding him based on the number of customer calls he handles. If the two conflict, guess which strategy he'll favor?

It's even better if you can tie the individual into a work group and reward all the group members based on the group's overall performance. Most work today is dependent on teamwork, so rewarding the entire group is a smart and powerful way to encourage everyone  to find ways to improve coordination, cooperation, and sharing. It's also a great method to entice your most productive people to help your least productive employees improve.

Specialized, Job-Specific Training

Here we're talking about teaching people how to do the kind of work you're asking for. So you'll offer training in equipment operations, in exercising the skills they'll use, and in understanding the information they'll use to do their best work.

TimeSaver
A valued worker with a proven commitment to the organization can be rewarded between review periods by giving him or her more decision-making responsibility. This empowers the individual, who can then make on-the-spot decisions, and at the same time frees the supervisor from being called in to make lower-level decisions when his or her time could best be spent elsewhere.

CASE IN POINT

In organizations where employees share in the profit potential, managers are increasingly turning many of the day-to-day decisions back to the employees—and with excellent results. In the retail industry, certain specialty department stores known for high standards of customer service, such as Nordstrom, expect their employees to mitigate the service with commonsense budget cutting. Since the employees share in the profits, they likewise have an incentive to cut costs. Thus, within certain parameters, it is left to each salesperson how best to do so.

Jerome, for example, is a sales associate in men's suits. During his workday, he interacts with over 200 potential customers, trying to offer each one excellent service. One customer, a local businessman, comes in to replace a favorite suit that is wearing thin. Jerome helps him locate the suit, sets him up with a fitter from alterations, and offers to deliver the suit. Jerome has closed the sale, has given up only five minutes over his lunch hour to deliver the package, and will undoubtedly see repeat sales from this satisfied customer.

Another customer, an up-and-coming professional woman, comes in looking for a birthday gift for her brother, who lives on the opposite coast. After much debate, she selects a pricey Italian linen shirt—in a trio of colors. Because Jerome wants to cultivate this woman as a regular customer, he decides to pull out all stops. Although the shirts came packaged from Italy, Jerome offers to have them pressed before gift wrapping so they arrive as crisp as possible. He also arranges door-to-door, next-day delivery at no charge to the customer. For a nominal alterations and overnight delivery charge, this customer leaves the store more than satisfied, and Jerome is pleased with his new client.

Profit Sharing

Increased Decisionmaking Power

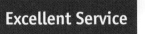
Excellent Service

Return Customers

RELATED TOPICS

➤ Using Praise to Get Results, (pages 48–49)

➤ Building Team Spirit, (pages 56–57)

➤ Motivation as a Daily Part of the Job, (pages 68–69)

Take a few minutes to evaluate each completed project with your delegates. Help them recognize what they did well, and where they may have room for improvement. It's also a good idea to help them recognize where no one could have foreseen a difficulty or unanticipated snag in the initial job plans.

Effective Delegation

As a supervisor or manager, it's an important part of your job to get work done through others. That makes delegation one of your primary methods, and one of your best ways to accomplish more every day.

In small work groups, you might thoroughly know each worker's unique skills and abilities. But when you supervise or manage more than half a dozen people, it's increasingly difficult to keep all their skills and work backgrounds in mind.

Here's a rundown of the steps required to consistently delegate as effectively as possible:

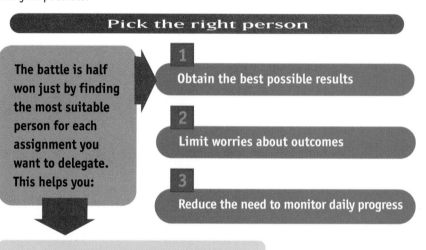

Pick the right person

The battle is half won just by finding the most suitable person for each assignment you want to delegate. This helps you:

1 Obtain the best possible results

2 Limit worries about outcomes

3 Reduce the need to monitor daily progress

Keep a written log of what people have done, and what skills they've shown you.

Set clear and objective goals

Delegation works best when both sides—you and your delegate—agree.

What's to be done

When it's due

What the limits are

What the budget permits

By communicating clearly, it'll be easier for your delegate to deliver. Establish a level of detail that encourages confidence in your delegate.

Devise a plan to monitor progress

Define goals for each meeting.

Keep close enough tabs on the project so that you'll recognize if it's veering off course, but don't "microman-age" or hover so that you annoy or interfere with your delegate's productivity.

Schedule a series of meetings when you initially dele-gate a task, and slate them at reg-ular intervals. The best interval is the longest period you can go while retaining a reason-able hope of fixing things if they come unglued.

Schedule meetings in advance. By doing so, you remove any impli-cation that you're not happy with your delegate's performance. How-ever, don't be afraid to call unscheduled meet-ings for tough issues if the situa-tion warrants.

RED ALERT! Be careful to give your dele-gate enough leeway to do things his or her own way. The extra freedom you per-mit will translate into addi-tional motivation to do a top-quality job. You'll also help your delegate gain more on-the-job experience and confidence.

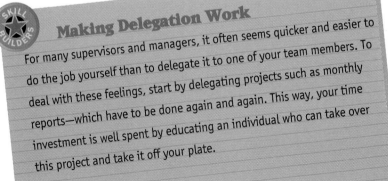

Making Delegation Work

For many supervisors and managers, it often seems quicker and easier to do the job yourself than to delegate it to one of your team members. To deal with these feelings, start by delegating projects such as monthly reports—which have to be done again and again. This way, your time investment is well spent by educating an individual who can take over this project and take it off your plate.

RELATED TOPICS

➤ Avoiding "Reverse" Delegation, (pages 12–13)

➤ Juggling Multiple Priorities, (pages 24–25)

Don't interpret reverse delegation as an effort by your team members to shirk their responsibilities. They often don't realize they're doing it. When you think it's appropriate, go ahead and accept some of their responsibilities. But always remain vigilant to the possibility of reverse delegation, particularly if you begin detecting a pattern of becoming overloaded with other people's work.

Avoiding "Reverse" Delegation

"Let me help you with that."

Earlier, you were introduced to some techniques for more effective delegation—but beware of the backlash. Savvy team members have been known to find ways to practice "reverse" delegation—the art of getting *you* to do the work you've assigned to *them*.

For example, suppose you delegate a financial analysis to one of your team members. The next day he asks how to calculate the cost of goods sold. Since it's a complicated task, you set up the formulas and punch in the numbers for him.

On the second day he's not sure how many scenarios to run or how to present the results. During the next half hour you make most of those decisions yourself.

On the third day, he reports that everyone's too busy to help him with the printing and stapling of his completed reports. You skip lunch to get him started, and eventually spend three more hours on what was supposed to be his project.

This sort of reverse delegation not only interferes with your own schedule and priorities but also wastes the organization's resources by pushing simple tasks and decisions *up* to a higher level of authority.

To keep yourself from becoming a victim of reverse delegation, make sure you:

Refuse to Be Taken

Since the people who work for you have no authority to give you assignments, they can't use reverse delegation unless they trick you or trap you into volunteering. So the best defense is what recruits learn rapidly in the army: *Never Volunteer!*

Avoiding Reverse Delegation

When a delegate asks you for a decision, don't make one. Instead, go over the various possibilities—with all their pros and cons—and return the decision-making task to the delegate.

If one of your team members complains that the task you've delegated is too uncertain, offer him or her additional training or suggest teamwork approaches with someone more experienced.

If the person who has responsibility for the task appears too inexperienced or otherwise unable to carry things forward, assign other team members to help.

When you're asked to pitch in and help, exit gracefully by pointing to all your other high-priority work.

Always Return the Other's Serve

The success of reverse delegation depends on the other person hitting a serve your way and hoping the ball stays in your court. You can defeat it, therefore, by returning other people's serves at the end of every conversation.

In practical terms, this means that whenever you break off a discussion or a conversation, mentally check to see who is responsible for taking the next step. And if it's you, say or do something that switches the responsibility to the other person.

For example, if your delegate starts walking away saying "So I'll get that information from you later today," you should suspect reverse delegation. To defeat such a tactic, reply with something like "I have a better idea. It will be faster if you go and get it yourself right now."

RELATED TOPICS

➤ **Effective Delegation,** (pages 10–11)

You might have your own ideas on how to collect and arrange the various processes and tasks involved in accomplishing your team's work. You might also be bound by established divisions of labor, tradition, union regulations, and other concerns.

However you divide the work—even if you simply retain the status quo—it's important to examine every job and make sure there's a reasonable chance the work regularly assigned to it can be carried out successfully.

WORDS TO LIVE BY

"A good manager is a man who isn't worried about his own career but rather the careers of those who work for him."

—H. S. M. Burns

Job Evaluation

One of the least understood but most fundamental responsibilities of a supervisor or manager is to look at the work under his or her authority and determine whether it's properly organized and arranged so that it can be accomplished at a satisfactory level.

This kind of "job evaluation" doesn't have to be done too often. But you should go through the exercise every time you take over a new area, every time you accept an important new responsibility, every time a reorganization reshuffles established responsibilities and work flow, and—even if none of these circumstances occurs—at least once every couple of years, just to be sure.

Job Evaluation Process

1 **Plot the work moving through your area.**
Consider and list all the inputs and outputs you supervise or manage every day. Inputs consist of work orders, raw materials, instructions from your boss, regulatory constraints, and everything else that dictates what you must try to accomplish. Outputs consist of your deliverables, the tangible products and services your team produces, as well as the "look and feel" you're expected to maintain within your area of responsibility.

2 Identify the work processes.

Between these inputs and outputs are the processes you oversee and control as you do your job every day.

Say, for example, your job involves the production of widgets. They probably enter your area as raw materials, go through various production processes, and leave as finished products packed in sturdy shipping containers.

Every stage the widgets go through—from receiving through milling and assembly right up to and including being packed for shipping—consists of one or more specific processes your employees perform. Some of these processes are entirely separate—like painting the finished widget red—but others are more interrelated with other processes—like bolting the two halves of the widget together.

This bolting process requires that the widget-halves have holes, that the holes line up, that the bolts have corresponding nuts, that all size specifications are met, and that all these elements come together at the right place and time with the proper tools and skills so that they can be bolted.

3 Collect and align related processes and tasks.

You could have the widget painted, then drilled and assembled, but it's probably more sensible to do the assembling first and then the painting.

As the work moves from its earliest to its final stages, there are numerous possibilities for how best to organize the necessary processes and tasks. In fact, there are arguments and evidence in favor of many conflicting arrangements.

For example, on automobile assembly lines, some workers claim that the best method is to move the engine around to different stations and let specialists each do a small part of the total job. But others argue that better engines are produced when one person or a small team builds a complete engine from start to finish.

Clearly, certain work—like racecar driving—is best done by individuals, while other work—like pit stops to add fuel and change tires—is best done by a group.

RELATED TOPICS

➤ Setting Goals (pages 26–27)

➤ Interviewing and Hiring (pages 32–33)

Preparing Accurate Job Descriptions

Most supervisors and managers acknowledge the need for clear, written job requirements before they interview and hire to fill these positions. Clearly stated requirements help interviewers cover all the appropriate topics with all the candidates.

In addition, experienced managers realize that accurate job descriptions are useful tools for increasing efficiency through better management.

As the work under your authority changes, and as you reorganize it to meet changing conditions, it's normal for specific positions to gain new responsibilities and shed old ones. Unfortunately, the written job descriptions for these positions rarely keep up with the day-to-day practical changes taking place. As a result, job descriptions are normally out of synch with the work people are actually doing.

SILICON AMERICA, INC.

We have started construction on our new plant in Hillsboro Creek by the Hillsboro Airport. Our project team has reached the stage where we need additional technical personnel to ensure the success of a state-of-the-art wafer manufacturing plant. We are interested in highly motivated and dedicated people for these positions. We are committed to provide you the environment and resources for success in your career and the plant. These are key positions in a startup of our new plant in Hillsboro.

We are interested in filling the following positions at this time.

ENVIRONMENTAL ENGINEER

This position will be responsible for all aspects of environmental and safety issues for the plant. This position will offer direct access to management and is looking for a proactive person who desires to maintain our plant environmental systems in the best condition and oversee plant safety. A BS degree in Environmental or related filed required. Environmental and code based experience a must. Knowledge of environmental and safety laws a must. This position will work with the Environmental Engineers at our Design firm through the build stage to an operational plant. Must have experience in waste water treatment, scrubbers, chemicals, reactive gases and doping gases.

CHEMICAL OR MECHANICAL ENGINEER

This is an equipment engineering position responsible for the wet processing equipment, chemical delivery systems, overseeing the bulk, reactive and dopant gas systems, RODI, scrubbers, waste water treatment system. BS in

Advantages to Accurate Job Descriptions

When filling the position: Evaluating the strengths and weaknesses of applicants becomes far easier and more relevant.

When reviewing employee performance: Performance evaluations and determinations about requirements for additional training become more accurate.

When revising or restructuring work: Finding the right position for a new responsibility or reorganizing an existing one becomes much easier.

Since millions of jobs have outdated, inadequate, or inaccurate job descriptions, it's likely you'll encounter the problem at some point in your career. How to respond? Don't panic, but don't ignore the problem, either. Just take the proper steps as discussed below to get those job descriptions updated and improved.

TimeSaver
Once you've got your job descriptions current, keep them that way. It's a lot easier and more efficient to review job descriptions once or twice a year and note recent changes than to go through this entire process again and again and again. Besides, accurate job descriptions make it easier to hire and manage people for the positions.

Keeping Job Descriptions Updated

Keep a log.
Ask people in each position to take notes on what they do for a day, a week, or a month. Once the log becomes repetitive, there's little value in continuing, so it's OK to use the shortest time period that contains the full scope of the position.

Calculate job requirements.
Examine the logs and note all the activities of the successful person in that position. Then list the skills and knowledge needed for each activity. For example: Contract preparation requires typing, familiarity with legal terms, and the ability to follow marked-up changes on early drafts. Client contact requires good communication and negotiation skills, as well as the ability to listen accurately and take careful notes.

RED ALERT! Be aware of job descriptions that diverge too far from reality. They often:
- include tasks that no longer need to be done.
- omit or deemphasize important but intangible skills.
- overemphasize just one part of the total job.

Check for thoroughness.
Any list can contain errors or omissions. To minimize these on your revised job descriptions, ask members of your team and even other supervisors to review the lists and offer comments. You might also want to add other tasks to a list if you feel it would be done by a person more qualified than whoever fills that position today.

RELATED TOPICS

➤ **Interviewing and Hiring, (pages 32–33)**
➤ **Compensation, (pages 36–37)**

Add narrative.
A simple list of activities and skills is useful, but it is further enhanced when accompanied by descriptions of what the person in this position actually does throughout the day. Include a chronology of actions, topics of conversations with others, and requirements for oral and written reporting.

Inside Info

It's rare that someone you supervise can fail all alone. Most of the time, it's important for *you*—as supervisor or manager—to take a share of the credit for the successes and blame for the failures of those you supervise. The sooner you begin to accept your own important role in other people's ability to follow the rules, learn more about their jobs, and achieve expected results, the sooner you can begin to evaluate each person's performance in its full context.

Writing a Performance Review

It's easy to base a judgment on a single impression. But evaluating an employee's performance involves much more than simply a "snapshot" of a person at work. Many supervisors and managers find the following four steps helpful in developing a performance review.

A Successful Performance Review

1 Meet with your employee to agree on specific performance goals over a certain period of time—the next three months, six months, or a year.

2 Keep a detailed record of individual accomplishments during this period.

3 Discuss his or her performance at the end of this period. Together, come to terms on the evaluations rating and discuss its implications.

4 Continue an open dialogue between yourself and the individual in which you can discuss remedying any deficiencies and improving important skills.

5 Offer training, education, counseling, closer cooperation, apprenticeship, or anything else you believe would support your employee's performance.

Tangible awards (such as trophies and raises) offer obvious incentive for hard work and improved performance and should be noted during any employee review. Ultimately, however, your job is to instill the belief that good work is its own best reward. Work closely with all of your employee to allow them to build a strong repertoire of skills and achievements that will make them feel better about their work. This will facilitate employee growth among those you supervise or manage.

Opening Lines of Communication

Get a better handle on performance evaluations by instituting "two-way" evaluations with people you supervise or manage. When you fill out rating sheets on employee progress, encourage them to fill out similar rating sheets on you. Then open the floor for them to share opinions of you as you share their your opinions of them. You'll not only become a better supervisor or manager through their criticisms, praise, and suggestions, but you'll also find new ways to improve your review process.

OPTICA Inc.
Employee Performance Review
1996

Employee: Cindy Farrell

Employee#: 145-23-1133

Hire D...

Performance Goals for Individual Employee's

1. Has he or she become a contributing member of the busi...
Cindy successfully planned a focus group series; resulting
implementation of new MagoCom campaign.

2. Can he or she handle local client's budgets?
She has restructured a local budget using the new spreadshee
software and is currently preparing a competitive analysis for
the southern regional office.

3. Is the employee able to present new concepts to clients?
On 2/10/96, Cindy prepared and presented the financial element
of the new campaign for MagoCom.

...e or she learned the newly installed accounting software?
...ificate for computer training was earned on 1/21/96.

...ments:
...essfully transitioned into the company and has
... be a valuable component of our business team.

... supportive in helping me articulate and
...oals.

A well-written performance review should outline the recent accomplishments of the employee, as well as improvements in job performance and new skills learned. It may also include visual information such as photos, videos, slides of completed projects, or graphs and charts that track performance. The evaluator should not focus on faults, but rather find a way to turn them around into opportunities for the employee to improve or enhance his or her skills. The review should be interactive, with the employee contributing self-observations of job performance and goals for the next review period.

RELATED TOPICS

➤ Giving Effective Feedback, (pages 46–47)

➤ The Advantages of Mentoring, (pages 70–71)

Placement Analysis

The other half of looking at the work under your authority is evaluating the individuals you supervise or manage to determine their qualifications for the position in which they're placed.

Since this involves a comparison between what real people can actually do and what ideal workers ought to be able to do, you'll need accurate job descriptions.

Placement Analysis

1 Itemize skills and abilities

For each person on your team, list what they do well, their areas of technical expertise, and the skills they have demonstrated.

Chris Morgan
1. Great team player.
2. Trains other employees well.
3. Detail-oriented and demonstrates problem-solving skills.
4. Creative managerial style!

2 Compare with job requirements

Compare each person's demonstrated skills and abilities against what the (accurate and recently updated) job description says a person in that position should be able to accomplish. This, of course, is the tricky part. On one hand, you don't want to make the mistake of discounting the excellent work of a proven performer because the job description says he should be able to do something extra—particularly if the job itself does not create much call for that skill or ability. On the other hand, you don't want to allow a smooth operator to continue winning high marks for doing only half the job that ought to be done. Making these judgments is one of the ways you earn your pay as a manager or supervisor.

"You have excellent leadership and teamwork skills, but we need. . ."

3 Consider the "intangibles"

These determinations contain an even larger "fudge" factor: the importance of intangibles. For example, suppose a salesperson has an unusually strong ability to make customers feel valued, important, and part of "the family." This may make him or her far better suited to a sales position than another person without this gift who matches all the objective requirements of the job description.

"The way you handled the V.P. at Franklin . . . remarkable job!"

Gathering Employee Feedback

Often, the most valuable tool to use when conducting a placement analysis is employee feedback. Most employees are drawn to position for which they have a natural aptitude. Ask your employees the following questions:

- Are you happy in the department/position you're currently in?
- Do you feel challenged in your current position?
- What are your short- and long-term work goals?
- How do you think your energy and expertise could be best utilized?

RELATED TOPICS

➤ Interviewing and Hiring, (pages 32-33)

Running Better Meetings

Inside Info

Meetings are only as useful as the results they produce. That's why it's critical to use meeting time to assign responsibilities, clarify your team's ideas and input, and create an action schedule for follow-up. If the meeting isn't utilized to achieve these goals, you'll have to contact the same people again later on to do what you could have done quickly and easily in the meeting.

One central task in supervising and managing people is conducting meetings. Whether you're talking to a single person on a single topic or your entire team on wide-ranging issues of policy and strategy, you're nevertheless consuming people's time in an effort to convey information and change behavior. The more effectively you can do this, the better you'll be able to perform your job.

Here are some fundamental techniques for getting more results out of every minute you and members of your team invest in meetings:

Prepare a Written Agenda

If you can't put one together for a meeting, you shouldn't hold the meeting—since you don't have a clear idea of what you want to accomplish. If, however, your goals for the meeting are firmly in place, you have a solid agenda that will help you succeed.

Before you put an item on a meeting's agenda, think it through. Have you done the groundwork to determine the facts, understand the issues, and be able to present the situation effectively to your team? If you're asking for input, have you given the people who will be at the meeting enough advance warning and information to develop meaningful suggestions and ideas?

WORDS TO LIVE BY

"Eighty percent of success is showing up."
—Woody Allen

Begin and End the Meeting on Schedule

It's rude to be late to a meeting. And it's equally rude—and an annoying penalty—to those who arrived on time for you to delay the start of the meeting to accommodate those who didn't.

There are two big advantages to stopping your meetings on time. First, knowing you have limited time provides both a structure and an incentive to keep the discussion moving forward at a good pace. Without a clear cut-off point, the whole meeting can become a leisurely exercise rather than an efficient tool of doing business.

Second, the inflexible closing deadline for the meeting forces you to allocate time according to the priority and importance of the subject under discussion. Small, simple decisions can—and should— be made in a few minutes, for example, in order to leave time for ample discussion of the bigger, more pertinent issues.

TimeSaver
No one likes a meeting that goes on forever, even if it accomplishes a lot. When creating your agenda, factor in an ending time for the meeting and then block out each item accordingly to cover every item on the agenda. If certain points need further discussion, suggest a later meeting where only the involved employees attend—freeing the rest up to move on to other things.

Follow the Agenda

Since your agenda is a basic plan for conducting the meeting more effectively, you might as well follow it. Take the agenda items in order. Check them off when completed. Avoid taking up new items of business that are not on the agenda unless you absolutely feel they are more important than the agenda items you have originally scheduled.

It's a good idea to use the written agenda for taking notes, jotting down assignments and deadlines, and otherwise keeping a record of what results from the meeting. This will greatly simplify the preparation of a follow-up report later on.

RELATED TOPICS

➤ Giving Effective Feedback, (pages 46–47)

➤ Resolving Conflicts Effectively, (pages 88–89)

Juggling Multiple Priorities

Inside Info

Don't give in to the natural tendency to work longer hours and weekends during crunch times. There's always a limit to your available hours. Instead, concentrate on finding ways to work smarter, *not* harder.

In other words, simplify what you must do, look for opportunities to accomplish two things at once, and carefully plan your schedule to make the most efficient use of your time and resources. An hour of planning nearly always does more good than two hours of unplanned effort.

WORDS TO LIVE BY

"All progress has resulted from people who took unpopular positions."

—Adlai Stevenson

nless you're supervising or managing just one person, it's inevitable you'll have to deal with a number of different tasks and assignments, all with conflicting and differing priorities and levels of importance.

Just keeping all these balls in the air requires great skill and attention to detail—without losing the big picture of what you're trying to accomplish and why! To help you, here are some suggestions from experienced supervisors and managers:

Take Shortcuts

Think back to a time when you faced a deadline and managed to accomplish a specific task in half the time you thought you'd need. That's the way to operate on all things you do during a particularly bad "crunch time."

Generally, you can do this by cutting corners on the less crucial tasks, by working at a faster pace with fewer breaks, by having more people assist you, and even by recycling some or all of the similar work you've done before.

Apply these principles to all your current tasks when you're under intense pressure, and you'll often be able to clear your desk of some high priority assignments in far less time than you thought they'd take.

Build Your Motivation Level

It's certainly important to focus on what must be done—and why. But it's equally important to jack up the level of your performance by increasing your desire and enthusiasm.

If you overwork yourself, you can easily begin to feel depressed and take a "what's the point" view of what you're trying to accomplish. To prevent this, include activities during even the tightest "crunch time" that improve your morale and build your motivation.

For example, schedule enough time for adequate sleep. Otherwise, your ability to work hard and make difficult decisions under pressure will be weakened. Also include regular reviews of how much you've accomplished in the last days and weeks of your over-crowded work schedule. Looking back will strengthen your ability to move forward and build your motivation level.

Focus on Critical Items

When the pressure to accomplish more in a short time begins to rise, respond by narrowing your attention to what's *most* important.

Cut back on the time you and your team spend on routine administrative and mainte-nance activities. Put these less critical tasks on a back burner and devote all your attention to accomplishing those of highest priority.

For example, postpone any routines you can safely delay, put off or dump meetings that have no urgent pur-poses, cut through the red tape you usually honor, and let others take on more of your responsibilities so you have more time to deal with the meat and bones of doing business.

Prioritizing

An easy way to establish your priorities is to make three separate lists, an "A," "B," and "C" list. On the "A" list, write down items that need to be addressed that day. On "B," list the assignments that can wait a day or two. The "C" list should include long-term or large projects that need time for preparation.

During the day, check off items from the "A" list and add new projects to appropriate lists as they come along. Don't forget the items on your "C" list; make sure to make daily progress on these goals, so the deadlines don't sneak up on you.

RELATED TOPICS

➤ **Effective Delegation,** (pages 10–11)

➤ **Maintaining Output with Minimal Staff,** (pages 62–63)

Setting Goals

In politics, leaders often determine which way the wind is blowing and which way the crowd is surging, then run around to position themselves at the head of the parade. In management and supervision, however, much more is involved.

You must be the real leader. Whether you take direction from above or you are the one at the top, it's up to you to provide leadership and goals not only for those who look to you for management and supervision but also for yourself—and particularly for your own career.

What's more, the closer you are to the front-line activity—actually providing services and dealing daily with customers—the more important it is for you to translate high-level goals and strategic objectives into day-to-day activities you can do yourself, and coach others into doing.

Some basic techniques for having and reaching results-oriented and satisfying goals include:

Make long-term projections

The best personal goals are those that will ultimately take you to a career level and life-style that interests and satisfies you. The best organizational goals are those that will enable you to reach the highest possible performance and success levels. Either way, you need longer-term goals than many people would concern themselves with.

To find these goals, just look farther ahead. Look around at your peers and competitors, and also at new opportunities, and consider where you—or the organization—would like to be five to ten years from now.

Create a one-year goal plan

Starting with these longer-term goals, work backward to see what ought to be accomplished in the coming year to put you on the proper pace. Include specific objectives with measurable criteria, so you—or anyone—can tell when you reach those objectives.

It's not worthwhile planning the second year, because at this point you don't know how much you'll do during the first twelve months.

Current Administrative PLAN

Break down plans into activities

People need shorter-term goals to provide guidance on a day-to-day basis. So use your one-year goals to develop monthly performance targets and, from them, weekly and daily lists of activities. Try to break the tasks down to a specific list of what to do each day.

This Year's Department Goals

Increased Customer Satisfaction

Monthly Department Goals

Attend Sales and Customer Service Workshops

Attend In-depth Product Orientation Classes

Daily Department Goals

1. Address Service Problems
2. Give Unsolicited Advice on Products

1. Give Unsolicited Information on Upcoming Products
2. Say "Thank You"

Block time for goal-related work

Don't block out all your time, of course, because shorter-term problems, issues, and concerns will crop up and demand your immediate attention; but *do* put at least one hour per day toward your longer-term goals, and over a year you'll make significant progress.

TimeSaver
When setting goals, whether short- or long-term, make sure to factor in the goals of your supervisor as well, to ensure that you're setting appropriate, approved goals for the organization.

RED ALERT!

One of the worst mistakes people make is to work on projects that seem important, even though they don't lead you toward your important longer-term goals. Instead, try to determine what "goal" each of your daily activities is supporting. Use these goals to help set relative priorities for daily tasks. If you don't know *why* you're doing something, stop and reflect.

RELATED TOPICS

▶ Giving Team Members More Effective Roles to Play, (pages 58–59)

Using Temps Effectively

Inside Info

Working with temporaries makes it easier to accept "flexible" job scheduling. The agency can take care of pairing people so you get Joe working mornings and Bill working afternoons, or Sally working three days a week and Linda two days a week, or whatever other combinations make sense.

At first, temporary employees were primarily used as stop-gap measures to fill in for regular employees on leave or to throw more bodies at a huge amount of work in an attempt to cope with a high-season crunch.

Currently, however, through adept marketing efforts by the largest temporary employment agencies, more and more employers are recognizing that the use of temporary employees can make a permanent contribution to profits.

In fact, nearly 25 percent of the new jobs being added to the U.S. economy are provided through temporary agencies, and "temps" now make up as many as 10 percent of all employees.

> **Here are some of the ways that savvy supervisors and managers are using temporary employees to increase their overall effectiveness:**

During the probationary period

Many employers are avoiding the commitment to untested work candidates by not hiring them but, instead, obtaining them as "temporary" workers.

Under this arrangement, you send the candidate to a temporary agency, with instructions that he or she is to be hired and sent back to you for work. Although you maintain full control over the new employee's hours, assignments, and pay rates, he or she actually "works for" the temporary agency.

If the new employee doesn't work out well or you discover after a few months that you have no need for his or her services, you can dismiss the employee with no further commitment. If, on the other hand, you like how well they perform, you can hire them directly.

PASSED

As a pool of skilled workers

Employers who experience strong seasonal patterns in their work loads—such as retail—find temporary employees an important supplement to a core group of full-time employees.

Due to family situations and other circumstances, many people don't want to work 12 months a year. They're happy to be part of a pool of skilled, trained workers that you hire regularly for short periods of time.

Call 1-800-ELF-TEMP

To cut administrative overhead

Some progressive temporary agencies have branched out into "renting" employees, whereby you write one check to the temp agency who then takes care of paying your employees, contributing to their retirement plans, paying the necessary employment taxes, and filing the regulatory paperwork.

Temps for Rent

RED ALERT!

Some work can be done by just about any "warm body." Other work requires general skills like typing and perhaps some desktop publishing experience. Finally, there are jobs that require highly specialized skills. Make sure the temporaries that come to you are not randomly "plucked" from the agency's pool. Instead, utilize agencies that will selectively fill your positions with skill-appropriate temps.

Once you find a few temps who work out well for you, request them by name the next time you need someone to fill in at an important job slot.

RELATED TOPICS

➤ Handling the Problems of Downsizing, (pages 60–61)

➤ Handling Decentralized and Flexible Work Groups, (pages 64–65)

When Employees Discuss Sensitive Matters

People on the job are, of course, just people. And they'll want to talk about a lot of sensitive issues: money, sex, politics, religion, race, and more. In general, placing tight restrictions on "approved topics of conversation" is not a wise idea. Such prohibitions tend to create resentment and only make the forbidden fruit more appealing.

But neither can you—as a responsible supervisor—permit the talk to veer off in any direction, or let it drain too much time and energy from the primary goals of accomplishing work and achieving objectives.

Here, then, are four guidelines to help you keep "on the job" conversation within reasonable bounds:

"Loose Lips Sink Ships"

This World War II slogan has a lot of meaning, even today. The more you—as supervisor or manager—discuss sensitive issues, the more opportunities there are for problems. Why? For two reasons:

- Even the gentlest comments on sensitive topics—coming from *you*—carry a much larger impact than they would coming from anyone else. It's best to stay as neutral and objective as possible, and to avoid presenting your opinions as the "right" ones.
- The more you talk about these issues, the more license you give others to talk about them, too.

Make Fun, Not War

Ponderous, intellectual discussions can harm a team's productivity, but an occasional good-natured joke or lighthearted comment can actually help build morale and enthusiasm.

One person's joke is another person's political dynamite, however, so stay on top of your team! Make sure they know the importance of not attacking each other's cherished beliefs or opinions on sensitive issues.

Prevent Preaching

One common feature of an uncontrolled workplace is "the preacher," a person with strong beliefs who feels he or she has the right *and* the obligation to convert everyone else on the job. This is a dangerous and counterproductive situation.

To avoid this potential predicament, strictly enforce "no preaching" rules equally against everyone who wants to sway others regarding politics, religion, social problems, health and diet, or any other sensitive matter.

People who want to learn more about someone else's beliefs can do so away from the job.

Put Policies in Place

RED ALERT!

A little bit of innocent, good-spirited political talk is natural in smoothly-functioning teams. But as soon as one person begins to advance the wrong amount or kind of talk—racism, sexism, blaming whole groups for general problems, and so forth—it's important to immediately step in and call a halt to this inappropriate behavior. Otherwise, you're asking for short-, medium-, and long-term problems.

We're seeing more and more lawsuits alleging that supervisors and managers have allowed political harassment or discrimination to occur on the job. To avoid this, you must make policies—perhaps even before you realize you need them.

The idea is to set forth rules and regulations that prevent anyone from making others feel uncomfortable on a sensitive issue. This can include everything from racial animosity to sarcastic criticisms of others' opinions. Keeping a tight rein on the one or two problem-talkers can often prevent a major drain on your entire team's productivity.

RELATED TOPICS

➤ **Handling Rebellious or Negative Employees,** (pages 78–79)

➤ **Resolving Conflicts Effectively,** (pages 88–89)

Inside Info

Many supervisors and managers fear the interview process because they don't properly prepare for it and then feel insecure about making a sound decision. In reality, though, and with practice, it's easy to select a qualified candidate. If you speak openly about relevant issues such as personality and motivation and thoroughly check references before making any hiring commitment, chances are you'll find an appropriate match for the organization.

WORDS TO LIVE BY

"It's all in the ear of the beholder."
—Tom Hayden

Interviewing and Hiring

Outstanding supervisors and managers often have one skill that sets them apart: the ability to spot good candidates for job openings. This skill pays off two ways:

First, not hiring problem employees is the easiest way to prevent headaches later on. Alcoholism, theft, tardiness, and turnover are rarely induced in good employees—they're brought with them to the workplace by problem employees who are hired without the use of good judgment.

Second, grabbing all the hard-working, highly motivated candidates you see is a great way to upgrade the baseline productivity and morale of any team.

Why more people don't have this skill is a mystery, because it's one that's fairly easy to acquire.

To improve your ability to interview and hire top quality candidates, begin with an accurate description of the job in question.

Interviewing and Hiring Guidelines

1 Ask pointed questions. Why bother with simple questions about expected topics? Most candidates have "canned" answers ready and you won't learn much. Instead, probe for the candidates' deeper motivations, values, and ambitions.

The best way is by asking about the candidate's first experiences with jobs, bosses, and successes. Details they share about what they did and didn't like will reveal a great deal to anyone who simply listens.

2 Take people at their word. If a candidate tells you "I couldn't stand all the crazy complaints customers came in with," you'll know he or she is not suited for a customer service position. Takes notes on what the candidate says, and look them over later to see where the candidate might be strong, or weak.

3 Hire for personality and aptitude; train for skills. In basketball, coaches know you can't teach height. In the same way, you can't teach an employee to be pleasant, interested in people, and warm. So hire the people who have the attitudes and personality traits you want, and concentrate your training on the skills they'll need to succeed on the job.

For example, an outgoing person can learn to do a receptionist's job. Eventually, you'll have a warm, friendly receptionist. That' better than hiring a grumpy misanthrope who happened to show up with receptionist skills at the ready.

RED ALERT!

Take unsupported assertions with a grain of salt. Just because a candidate's résumé states that he or she was president of ITT, you shouldn't believe it without checking. Surveys show that blatant lying—or simply "stretching the facts"—on résumés and applications is not only prevalent but at an all-time high. Use your judgment to assess the person, and then check their qualifications before you make a hiring decision.

Résumé and Work History
Greg Michaels
144 N. Cerritos Avenue
Glendale, California 91206

Objective:
To gain a progressive management position in active sportswear, marketing, development, manufacturing, or public relations.

Experience:
Portfolio Analyst
Smith Barney, Inc.
                                                              1994 to Present
                                                                        Los Angeles, California
Experienced in financial analysis of corporations, individuals, and product lines. Developing and providing service to a wide-reaching client base, with an emphasis in technology and consumer-based companies.

Product Management and Product Development
Royal Family, House of Windsor
                                                              1990–1994
                                                                        London, England
Coordinated the Royal Family fashion purchases in North America and Great Britain. Synchronized and staged highly personalized fashion shows and buys with various high-end New York and European fashion houses. Managed all financial aspects and logistical coordination for the Family, stressing the highest order of employer comfort and satisfaction.

Lexus, Toyota USA
Developed a signature line of apparel for Lexus and Toyota USA. Involved in all aspects of product management from design inception and sales forecasting to apparel production and delivery. Responsibilities included sourcing, tracking, and production liaison between manufacturing and customs houses. Managed on-site production specification inspections, cost pricing review, and productivity monitoring for timeline targeting.

Marketing Manager, Men's Active Sportswear
Atlas Clothing
                                                              1985-1990
                                                                        Seattle, Washington
Marketing manager of active sportswear clothing line that concentrated on life-style apparel. Planned and implemented marketing and sales strategies on both regional and national levels. Worked hand in hand with advertising agency to develop all media. Coordinated and mediated product focus groups, conducted consumer awareness campaigns, participated in various trade shows, and conducted retail sales presentations.

Manufacturing Sales Representative
Gear Shoes
                                                              1983–1985
                                                                        Dallas, Texas
Solicited new accounts in a defined sales territory and managed all aspects of established accounts. Represented manufacturers and various industry trade shows. Worked closely with buyers from major area retailers.

:
• Business unit manager
• Marketing/Sales
• Product development

cont.

RELATED TOPICS

➤ **Understanding Affirmative Action and EEOC,** (pages 40–41)

➤ **Effective Training Practices,** (pages 74–75)

Firing

In this day and age of "wrongful termination" lawsuits, the process of firing an unsatisfactory employee is best done "by the book." An effective supervisor or manager will adhere to the following steps in making this transition:

Start Early

In his old-time television show, George Burns used to fire Harry Von Zell every week with no warning. In those days, that was only partly a joke, and it was mostly funny because it was so close to the truth.

Today's employment laws generally prevent "on the spot" firing. Instead, supervisors must follow a mandated series of steps that provide the employee plenty of notice that he's headed down the wrong track and faces potential termination.

The only time you can act immediately is when certain specific situations arise: physical violence, criminality, arriving at work under the influence of drugs or alcohol, and so forth. Short of this, however, you'll need to take the proper steps to be sure the employee has no grounds for a costly lawsuit.

Explain the Problem

The firing process begins with a meeting between you and the problem employee where you explain the reason for the meeting—the behavior or incident that you think makes the employee a good candidate for "hitting the highway."

You also give the employee a chance to explain his or her side of the story and, if you were wrong or simply misinformed, make clear the mistake was yours and the worker is back to having a perfectly clean slate.

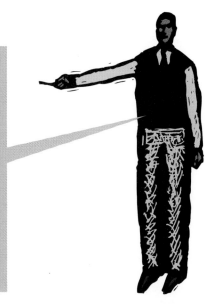

Document and Warn
At this initial meeting, you as supervisor have the option to formally warn the employee in writing, but you should do so only if you truly interpret the offense as severe enough to mandate this action. If not, you can use the first meeting as a "verbal warning," and then, if it becomes necessary, begin documentation of the same behavior from then on.

Each time the employee is late, absent without permission, performs unsatisfactorily, or exhibits inappropriate behavior, you should place another note in his or her employee file. In addition to informing the employee of the action you've taken, it's also a good idea to write a memo describing the problem behavior, date, time, context, and so forth, and have him or her sign a copy before you put it in the file.

 RED ALERT! Try not to get so wrapped up in the process of firing an employee that you fail to recognize a personal or work-related problem that may be adversely affecting the employee's work performance.

Offer a "Way Back"
At some point in this process, perhaps even at the first meeting, you should offer problem employees a chance to "straighten up and fly right"—in other words, an opportunity to modify the undesirable behavior.

In short, you tell them exactly what they must do to stop being problem employees. If they do it, you won't need to fire them. If they don't, at least you gave them a fair chance to avoid being fired. In this way, you have offered a "way back," a second chance.

WAY BACK   YOU'RE FIRED

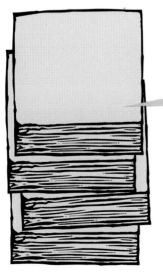

Build to a Crescendo
Let your documentation and warnings become more and more specific, frequent, and stringent regarding standards for future behavior. The goal here is to paint a picture of an employee who continues to go downhill over a period of weeks or months and does nothing to reform. At the proper moment, you're then justified in giving notice of termination.

RELATED TOPICS
➤ Writing a Performance Review, (pages 18–19)

Compensation

Pay is one of the most complex and emotional aspects with which supervisors and managers must deal. People rarely feel they're getting enough, and, indeed, compensation is often considered a "dirty little secret" that can't be discussed in public.

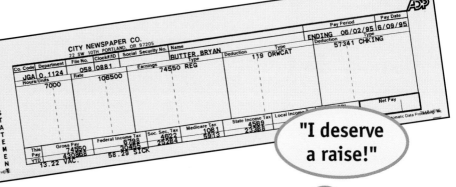

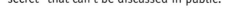

"I deserve a raise!"

Setting Pay

Establishing a particular employee's pay level depends on myriad factors, including pay equity, pay competitiveness, pay ranges, merit pay, and cost-of-living pay increases.

All these issues are only a part of what often makes "pay" a complicated issue. Justifiably or not, most people equate their pay level with the degree of success and appreciation they feel from their jobs. At higher levels, people allow pay to become the basis for their feelings of self-worth.

Talking Pay

Despite the complexity and emotionalism, you need to be able to discuss and set pay levels. Simply put, this is an important part of being an effective supervisor or manager.

For example, you can use higher pay rates and on-the-spot increases to support your performance guidelines or to reward people who make special contributions to your team's success. If you lack the power or the budget to give raises during a certain period, you may find your team demotivated, unhappy, and looking elsewhere for other opportunities.

WORDS TO LIVE BY

"Wages are the measure of dignity that society puts on a job."

—Johnnie Tillmon

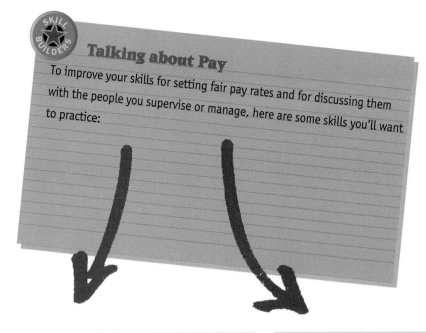

Talking about Pay

To improve your skills for setting fair pay rates and for discussing them with the people you supervise or manage, here are some skills you'll want to practice:

RED ALERT! Because talking about pay and dealing with compensation issues are such vital parts of your job as a supervisor or manager, you can't let emotional squeamishness get the better of you. Learn to interact openly with your employees on these issues. Just as you eventually learned the skills of driving a car, or swimming, you can also develop the supervisory skills of communicating effectively about pay issues.

Ease the stress

- Before you make a decision or talk to anyone about pay, do some research on the relevant facts. Check the employee's history of pay levels, performance, and whatever else may be relevant. If you feel sure about the facts, you'll have one less thing to be nervous about.

- Talk in private. Other people only add to the stress level. But keep an interpreter or union representative in the meeting, if necessary.

- Be very personal. Start with easy conversation about friends and family. After a few minutes of developing a better comfort level, talk about pay won't seem so stark and foreboding.

- Smile and listen at least as much as you talk. This reciprocal and nonverbal behavior will help to reduce the employee's anxiety level and will also leave you open to hear exactly what he or she is trying to tell you.

Don't pull your punches

- Be open about the good or bad news.

- Use specific facts and figures. Generalities only create confusion and anxiety.

- Don't bring up the employee's past mistakes as a ploy for deferring the issue. Negotiate in good faith by acknowledging the individual's accomplishments and by rewarding them.

- Make no promises, unless you're absolutely sure you can deliver on them. A broken promise about pay is not only demotivating, it's an invitation to a lawsuit.

RELATED TOPICS

➤ **Distributing Non-monetary Rewards,** (pages 50–51)

Inside Info

Be realistic when evaluating employee performance. Don't praise or blame without a solid reason. If you should later decide to discipline or discharge an employee, you'll be in better shape by having a paper trail that supports your actions.

Avoiding Legal Actions

Today there is an entire web of local, state, and federal laws that cover the workplace. Every important action is covered, one way or another. As a supervisor or manager, you must act in accordance with all of these laws or you risk bringing down heavy penalties on your organization.

Short of obtaining a law degree, your best bet is to follow some simple, tested principles. The five most important are:

1 When hiring, give every qualified candidate a fair chance to be evaluated. It's against the law to ask about health conditions and disabilities or to test for illegal substances. However, you can verify that immigrants applying for work have the proper authorizations and paperwork.

Job Application

2 It's illegal in every workplace-related situation to make judgments or treat people differently solely because of their race, ethnicity, gender, age, religion, national origin, marital or parental status, illness or disability. So make sure you apply the same standards to everyone when handing out rewards, perks, assignments, or evaluations.

Also, do your best to prevent employees from making jokes, slurs, or demeaning remarks, and from using body language or exhibiting other behavior that other employees could interpret as intimidating or antagonistic.

WORDS TO LIVE BY

"Laws are felt only when the individual comes into conflict with them."

—Suzanne LaFollette

3 Sexual discrimination is a particularly serious form of bias and discrimination that should be eradicated. The main criterion for sexual discrimination is not what people do, but how people *perceive* what is done. Thus, women who feel respected and well-liked are far more tolerant of jokes and bantering than women who feel taken advantage of or unappreciated.

Certain hiring determinations based on gender are, of course, justified. For example, it's not considered sexual discrimination for a woman to get the job of Snow White in a Disneyland production; but it would be a factor if she was not hired as a tour guide or security guard simply on the basis of her sex.

RED ALERT! **P**rivacy lawsuits are becoming increasingly commonplace. You can defend your organization far better against them if you write a simple paragraph for your employee handbook which says—in appropriate language that reflects your states legal statutes—that workplace equipment and facilities are subject to search and surveillance at any time.

The law recognizes two main categories of sexual harassment:

- Quid pro quo involves asking for sexual favors in return for providing something else: a raise, a promotion, or just keeping one's job.

- Hostile environments are less distinct. Basically, anything that a woman perceives as hostile in the workplace—from pin-up calendars to unwanted touching—can become grounds for a lawsuit.

4 Make no promises unless you're certain you can keep them. Under present interpretations of the law, even an innocent comment from a supervisor or manager can become the basis of a binding employment contract.

"Get this project done on time and there's a big bonus for you..."

5 Maintain written policies documenting everything of importance, particularly attendance, tardiness, and use of company equipment such as telephones and computers. This gives you the upper hand if the time comes to defend your organization against legal claims for damage or unfair treatment.

Company Handbook

RELATED TOPICS

➤ **Understanding Affirmative Action and EEOC,** (pages 40–41)

➤ **Dealing with Sexual Harassment,** (pages 42–43)

Inside Info

As a supervisor or manager, your personal attitude can make or break your organization's Equal Employment Opportunity and affirmative action policies. Whatever your opinion, you owe it to your team and your organization as a whole to honor and implement these policies as best you can.

Remember: Nothing in the affirmative action laws require or even suggest that individuals be hired, promoted, or protected against layoffs if they are not qualified to perform their jobs.

WORDS TO LIVE BY

"The Constitution does not provide for first and second class citizens."

—Wendell L. Willkie

Understanding Affirmative Action and EEOC

Despite the rhetoric from people both for and against affirmative action and equal employment opportunity laws, the basic concepts surrounding them are not nearly as controversial as many people would have you believe.

Here is a brief summary of what your organization should be doing:

Carefully Examine Your Workforce

The laws are intended to open a fair level of opportunities for everyone available to work. To verify if you are in compliance, check your present workforce for what's called "underutilization." If you have a certain job or position filled with fewer members of any religious, cultural, gender, or ethnic group than one might

reasonably expect based on their numerical availability, then there's a possibility that you might be in violation.

Whenever you identify a job that has underutilization, the regulators expect you to take special steps—over a period of time—to hire more members of the underrepresented group.

RED ALERT!

The wrong attitudes toward any group of people can undermine the best-intentioned Affirmative Action efforts. That's why you should monitor not only your own attitudes but also those of your team members regarding outsiders.

Be alert for any suggestion that members of certain groups are less capable, less devoted to the job, less willing to accept responsibility, or less deserving of high pay than other groups.

Also watch for people who feel certain groups are less intelligent, less easily accepted by others, or less productive than others.

Look for obvious segregation in the workplace, open telling of offensive ethnic jokes, different salary scales for different groups doing the same work, or inferior access for handicapped workers.

If you find any hint of such factors, react firmly and quickly with "sensitivity" or "diversity" training—as well as necessary remedial actions—to help your team achieve the benefits of a diverse but cohesive workforce.

Evaluate Possible Bias

Since your hiring capacities may be limited, each time you select one person to hire, members of every other group "lose out." It takes more than this, however, to establish bias. The following criteria should be used to analyze potential bias within your organization:

- What percentage of key decision makers are members of any one group?

- What percentage of management and supervisory trainees are members of any one group?

- What percentage of promotions go to members of any one group?

- What percentage of your organization's customer/client service positions are filled with members of any one group?

Answers higher than 50 percent may indicate your organization inadvertently offers members of one group more opportunities than members of other groups.

TimeSaver
Many people erroneously believe that these laws apply only to a few organizations. Actually, there are countless local, state, and federal laws regulating different aspects of job-related hiring, placement, training, promotion, compensation, termination, layoff, membership in a union, and more. It's faster and safer, therefore, to consider that your organization is probably covered, and to comply as best you can.

RELATED TOPICS

➤ Interviewing and Hiring, (pages 32–33)

➤ Supervising and Managing Diverse Groups, (pages 54–55)

Inside Info

Because it's far better to have an honest conversation about boundaries than to make simpleminded, inflexible lists of do's and don'ts, most experts advise that men and women be more willing to discuss the issue of sexual harassment, and try to negotiate more about what goes on in the work environment.

Dealing with Sexual Harassment

Sexual harassment is a particularly difficult problem to address—partly because nearly all male-female interactions are somewhat complex but more specifically because its definition includes the concept of "unwelcome" action.

In Hollywood, screenwriters want to generate maximum interest in a film about sexual harassment, so they put a man in a situation where he suffers from the cruelty and insensitivity of a beautiful woman. But, in reality, only 5 percent of sexual harassment complaints come from men. What's more, by some estimates as many as 15 percent of all the women employed by Fortune 500 companies suffer sexual harassment each year, including 1 percent who are sexually assaulted—physically attacked and hurt—each year, more often by managers and professionals than by hourly employees.

The law now defines two forms of sexual harassment: the *quid pro quo* form—where one party demands sexual favors in return for a promotion or raise, or even just keeping one's job, and the *hostile environment* form—where comments, leering, touching, sexual jokes, cheesecake photos, or other behavior can be enough to constitute harassment, regardless of intent. Under the hostile environment doctrine, all that's important is how the individual perceives the behavior.

The 1991 Civil Rights Act not only translated both forms of sexual harassment into illegal employment discrimination but also provided for punitive monetary damages. Women who truly are sexually harassed now have a form of recourse they didn't have before.

WORDS TO LIVE BY

"It is no use walking anywhere to preach unless our walking is our preaching."

—St. Francis of Assisi

RED ALERT!

With the exception of blatant behaviors like quid pro quo demands and any form of violence, factors like the context of behavior and the woman's perception of the man's intention become central to defining what is and is not sexual harassment.

That's why supervisors and managers should caution everyone to think more carefully about the impact of their behavior on others, making sure they have given the other person the opportunity to say "please stop what you are doing" without fear of later reprisals.

On the other hand, people who feel they are subject to sexual harassment should be as clear and firm as possible when warning the offending party that their behavior and/or comments are unwelcome. They should also avoid situations where they might give someone the wrong idea, like going to a private hotel room or a home instead of a public area for a meeting.

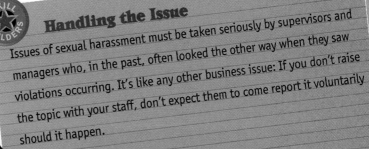

SKILL BUILDERS

Handling the Issue

Issues of sexual harassment must be taken seriously by supervisors and managers who, in the past, often looked the other way when they saw violations occurring. It's like any other business issue: If you don't raise the topic with your staff, don't expect them to come report it voluntarily should it happen.

RELATED TOPICS

➤ **Effective Training Practices, (pages 74–75)**

➤ **Resolving Conflicts Effectively, (pages 88–89)**

Inside Info

Violence can take on many forms, including verbal violence. Strong and threatening language can be just as intimidating as a punch in the nose—and the effects last longer. Stay aware of the risk of verbal violence in your organization and send out the message that violence—of any kind—will not be tolerated.

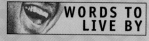

WORDS TO LIVE BY

"Violence seldom accomplishes permanent and desired results. Herein lies the futility of war"

—Asa Philip Randolph

Handling Violence in the Workplace

Workplace violence needn't always explode like a postal worker with a gun. It can involve a fistfight, a shove, or even an intimidating threat of force.

Workplace violence—in whatever form it takes—is potentially dangerous. People can be hurt. Productivity and morale are usually damaged. And the threat of a lawsuit by the victim of violence makes the whole situation costly for the company.

In the movies, the best method for handling violence is usually to suppress it with even stronger violence or the threat of violence. In the workplace, it's impractical—and ill-advised—for the supervisor or manager to play the role of Clint Eastwood. A far better approach is to spot the signposts of impending violence and to take action *before* it ever occurs.

Supervisors and managers are wise to become familiar with workplace situations that tend to produce the escalation of violence. The following guidelines can help you maintain a violence-free work environment.

Treat everyone with sensitivity and caring

Although most people will never "go off" like a time bomb in the workplace, it's very difficult to determine in advance who really might. Clinical studies show that some of the most explosive individuals display stable, lengthy workplace histories and very docile personalities. They often compile excellent attendance and work histories, too.

Rather than looking for "loose cannons" that might go off unexpectedly, focus your attention toward reducing violence by maintaining a consistently calming, anger-defusing attitude toward all of your employees.

Go easy on the dictates

Years ago, supervisors and managers tended to rely on an authoritarian manner in which they simply told each person what to do and when—but rarely why. Today we recognize that people respond with more enthusiasm and generate better results if supervisors and managers adopt a coaching, collaborative style.

As an extra benefit of this teamwork approach, coaching and collaboration tend to reduce the possibility that employees will bottle up their feelings. Without the old pattern of heavy-handed supervision, there's far less chance for an explosive reaction to day-to-day workplace activities and interactions. Statistics confirm that the suppression of emotions, rather than the loose expression of them, leads to workplace violence.

Keep an eye peeled

Encourage everyone in the workplace to keep an eye peeled for the possibility of violence. Employees don't need to be clinical psychologists to do this, either. Studies show that violence in the workplace rarely takes place like an "explosion." Instead, it's normally signaled well in advanced by a long series of increasingly unusual events. These might include emotional outbursts, confrontations with co-workers or authority figures, and non-violent but nevertheless antisocial activities.

Make clear that you want to be told about coworkers who show any unusual signs of anger, irritability, or emotional immaturity that might lead them into a situation where they feel there is "no way out."

RED ALERT!

If you sense a person has entered the beginning of the "cycle of violence," don't wait for the end of the progression before you decide to take preliminary action. Call your organization's human resources department immediately and seek a specialist who can provide some intervention and help.

One effective strategy is to offer the individual a few days of leave or vacation time. Days off from work can function like a "time out" to help defuse potential violence before it breaks out into overt behavior.

If you encounter a situation where real violence might erupt any minute, the best intervention might be to bring in some security personnel to protect coworkers from the potentially violent person.

RELATED TOPICS

▶ Reducing Stress Levels, (pages 76–77)

▶ Taming the Bully (pages 82–83)

Giving Effective Feedback

Among the skills that distinguish between average supervisors or managers and the most highly successful ones is the art of giving effective feedback.

Many people think putting a positive spin on their criticisms and suggestions is all they need do. But there's a lot more to converting good perceptions and ideas into effective feedback. Here are some points to practice:

Focus First on Actions

Rather than envisioning people as a mere collection of attributes and attitudes, the effective supervisor or manager knows it's far better to focus on specific behaviors.

Instead of telling an employee "you have the wrong attitude," begin to offer your feedback with a more practical opener, such as "you're giving the impression that you're impatient and uninterested."

Placing your emphasis on action instead of attitude makes it easier for the employee to accept what you're saying, and lets him or her concentrate on what to do to make the desired improvement.

Inside Info

Providing effective feedback to employees is one of the most important skills to foster because the normal chain of communication is always full of opportunities for errors and misunderstandings. In feedback, a small and simple miscommunication can change, or even reverse, the meaning of what you're saying.

The more accurately you say what you mean, the better the chance your feedback will have the impact you intend.

WORDS TO LIVE BY

"They that will not be counseled, cannot be helped. If you do not hear reason she will rap you on the knuckles."
—Benjamin Franklin

"You always create problems around here!"

"You have the wrong attitude."

Ineffective Feedback

Be Specific

It's very easy to say "you always create problems around here." But it's far more effective to specifically point out the incident in question, such as "yesterday at 3 P.M. when you were talking to Sally your voice was so loud that Sam, who was calling me from Seattle, asked about the disturbance."

If you're vague, there's far less assurance that you and the person to whom you're giving feedback are on the same mental page.

Be Supportive

If your feedback provokes anxiety, the other person will likely be demotivated to change in ways you want. So surround your ideas and suggestions with generous helpings of support.

A good pattern is to begin with a positive comment. Then offer your feedback and training or other resources to make it easier for your employee to make use of your recommendation.

It's also a good idea to occasionally offer positive feedback that simply acknowledges the employee's skills, creativity, and good results.

"You're giving the impression that you're impatient and uninterested."

"Yesterday at 3 P.M. when you were talking to Sally your voice was so loud that Sam, who was calling me from Seattle, asked about the disturbance."

Effective Feedback

RED ALERT!

Be careful not to let too much time elapse between the action that precipitates your decision to give some feedback and the moment you actually give it.

When it's fresh in both your mind and your employee's, there's less controversy about what actually happened, and the feedback has a better chance to take hold and produce positive changes.

RELATED TOPICS

➤ **The Advantages of Mentoring,** (pages 70–71)

➤ **Empowering Your Employees,** (pages 90–91)

Using Praise to Get Results

Inside Info

Don't get into the habit of giving empty praise. While it may provide you with temporary results, your employees will quickly see through the facade and will regard you as insincere.

Even though praise is free, most people are far too stingy with it. But used properly, it is a most powerful tool in the hands of a supervisor or manager who wants to become more effective. Here are some simple guidelines for how to use praise to achieve beneficial results in the workplace.

Praise Quickly

Praise that's kept too long in storage will quickly lose its sweetness and appeal. So get in the habit of offering simple, sincere bits of praise as soon as you observe praiseworthy actions taken by your employees.

Praise Often

If you think of it as a scarce commodity, you might not want to distribute praise very freely. But when you realize there are plenty of ripe opportunities to offer praise, you can begin to hand it out like candy at an elementary school picnic—and with much the same effect.

Praise Specifics

It's nice to say "you're doing a great job." But it's far more powerful to say something like "the way you handled that McComber problem this morning made me realize how much your skills have improved since last year."

By offering praise in a specific context, you've made personal contact, shown how much you know about the individual and the situation under discussion, and given your praise real power to elevate a person's motivation and enthusiasm.

"Good job keeping that squirrel outta here, Puddin!"

WORDS TO LIVE BY

"The service we render to others is really the rent we pay for our room on this earth . . . the purpose of this world is not 'to have and to hold' but 'to give and serve.' There can be no other meaning."

—Sir Wilfred T. Grenfell

Praise in Public

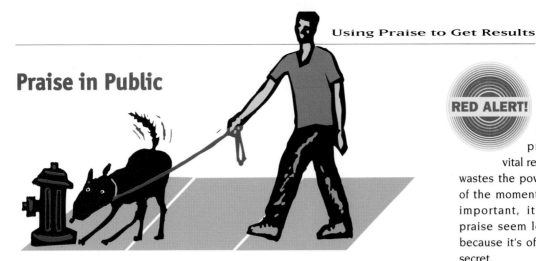

Try not to make the mistake of praising in private. One vital reason is that it wastes the powerful impact of the moment. Even more important, it makes the praise seem less valuable because it's offered only in secret.

Just as it's important to criticize and discipline in private, it's vital that you praise people in public. There are several reasons to do so:

First, praising in public gives the individual a double dose of good feeling. He or she gets the original good feeling directly from the praise you're offering. Then there's a second shot of good feeling because those who witness you praising him offer their own congratulations, pride, and joy.

Second, praising in public creates an opportunity for you to reward the whole team, not just the individual who most recently earned your admiration. So the individual's good effort gets reflected back to produce favorable results not only on him or her but also on everyone who works for you.

Finally, praising in public sends out the message that you indeed value the offering of praise. Others will want to receive praise from you and will try harder than ever to earn it.

TimeSaver
When setting goals, whether short- or long-term, make sure to factor in the goals of your supervisor, as well, to ensure that you're setting appropriate, approved goals for the organization.

Praise Whatever You Want More of

It's a good idea to praise anything and everything that approaches your vision for how you want the workplace and the team to operate. The general rule is that you'll get more of whatever you praise, so use your praise like a compass to guide your entire team toward implementing the systems, methods, procedures, and behaviors that you desire.

RELATED TOPICS

➤ **Building Team Spirit, (pages 56–57)**

➤ **Motivation as a Daily Part of the Job, (pages 68–69)**

Inside Info

Nonmonetary rewards can factor into employee negotiations, as well. For example, if you want to hire a sales representative but can't match the candidate's previous salary, you might choose to compensate in a non-monetary way—such as a company car or an expense account. Or, if you'd like to offer a stellar employee a promotion which your budget doesn't permit, you may choose to sweeten the offer with a bit of extra vacation time.

WORDS TO LIVE BY

"Solvency is entirely a matter of temperament and not of income."
—Logan Pearsall Smith

Distributing Nonmonetary Rewards

It's a myth that good employees only care about money. In reality, they're motivated by and satisfied with a whole range of nonmonetary rewards that you can provide at little or no cost.

Nonmonetary rewards can be anything and everything—both tangible and intangible— that an employee would like to receive.

Examples of tangible nonmonetary rewards include: leave time, early dismissal, extra vacation time, longer lunch hours, a better parking space, the employee's picture on the wall (perhaps under a sign: "Employee of the Week"), a nicer office location, more contemporary office furniture, and so forth.

Examples of intangible nonmonetary rewards include: teaming the employee with the person he or she would like to work closely with, offering the most exciting or challenging work assignments, giving more responsibility, allowing more flexibility in work schedules, supporting his or her request to do telecommuting, providing more training in new and interesting skills or technologies, supporting a request for transfer or promotion, and many others.

Here's how to get the most bang for every buck of non-monetary rewards you can offer:

Make sure the reward is justified

Just because you may provide employees with rewards that are non-monetary, there should nevertheless be "value" involved. Strictly control who receives the rewards. And, above all, before you give a reward, make sure the recipient has fulfilled whatever requirements you've set forth to earn it.

Openly announce the rewards

Just as you should praise in public, you should give these rewards in public, too. You'll get the same triple mileage from public distribution of nonmonetary rewards.

Be careful not to dispense nonmonetary awards too lavishly. Just because these rewards don't involve a cash outlay doesn't mean that they don't affect the organization's store of resources.

One reward at a time

Money is a single reward, and everyone understands it. That's why it's so powerful. Don't make matters overly complicated by jumping from one nonmonetary reward to another too quickly.

Of course, you should let your employees work toward the rewards they most want, so that they're motivated to the maximum extent possible. But by the same token keep your efforts to promote and emphasize the rewards simple by focusing on just one reward at a time.

TimeSaver

Behave as any smart negotiator would and prepare a list of nonmonetary items that you could or would be able to distribute among your employees. Then, when the need arises, you have a "bank" from which to draw on.

Practice fairness and consistency

Just as with pay considerations, it's crippling to your team's morale and enthusiasm for them to perceive you as arbitrary, unfair, or one to play favorites. Make sure you maintain the same degree of fairness and evenhandedness with your employees as you award nonmonetary rewards.

For instance, if Erwin earns a reserved parking space for a month because of some admirable work he does, then when Sally does the same amount and quality of work, she should also earn the right to use the reserved parking place. Don't give her half a day off from work, unless of course that's what she prefers.

RELATED TOPICS

➤ Compensation, (pages 36–37)

➤ Using Praise to Get Results, (pages 48–49)

Inside Info

Trimming the Power of the Grapevine

Your employees have a way of knowing what's going on. If they're concerned about takeover rumors, signs of impending layoffs, talk of profit problems, or other big issues, don't simply ignore the situation. Doing so will only provide more fertilizer to strengthen the grapevine.

Instead, be frank and open to the fullest extent of your knowledge. The more freely you share what you know with the people you supervise or manage, the more they'll trust what you tell them and respond to your requests.

Truth!!

To: Marcia   cc: Brad, Shaneeya

Address Book

Subj: Daryl and Tanya

Attach File

File: ☐ Return Receipt

Have you heard? Why am I always the last to know the good stuff? What is Meredith going to do to them? Yeoooow!!!

Send Later

LW

Send Now

The grapevine exists in every workplace, and more often than not it carries a lot of accurate information faster and easier than the more formal channels of information. Unfortunately, with equal facility, it also carries unfounded rumors and outright misinformation.

If you've ever made the attempt, you know that trying to destroy the grapevine, or ignore it, is a losing battle. But you can do a great deal to mitigate its negative impact on the people you supervise or manager. Here's how:

WORDS TO LIVE BY

"Gossip is news running ahead of itself in a red satin dress."
—Liz Smith

1 Provide more information

Grapevines thrive in dry conditions. The less you tell people about what's going on, the more branches the grapevine will develop, and the more people will nurture it.

Instead, kill the grapevine with large doses of truthful information. The more you say that rings true to people, the less they'll listen to whatever else the grapevine is telling them.

2 Correct incorrect rumors ASAP

Put out memos, post notices on bulletin boards, make announcements in meetings, and circulate newsletters or flyers, if necessary. In the face of false information, take whatever steps you feel are necessary to get corrected information to your employees as quickly as possible.

Every hour you delay gives the false information more time to take root and influence what your people are thinking, feeling, and doing on and off the job.

RED ALERT!

When a rumor is spreading thickest and fastest, your best bet for providing accurate information is to establish an "anti-rumor hotline." This can be a person or, in larger groups, a telephone number or computerized access point where people can obtain facts and information other than what the grapevine is providing.

3 Always give the facts

You may not give ALL the facts, ALL the time, but don't lie to the people you supervise or manage. Eventually your lies will be discovered, forever undermining your ability to influence, motivate, and lead the people on whom you depend to get your work accomplished.

If you lack complete information, it's OK—and advisable—to say so. People can tell when they're getting a snow job, and when they're not, they're remarkably supportive and willing to wait.

4 Favor face-to-face meetings

The more important and potentially upsetting the news you want to share, the more crucial it is that you share it personally. People don't take kindly to negative information they get secondhand, in printed form, or over the loudspeaker. Of course, they may not like to hear it much in person, either, but at least there's the potential to forge a stronger relationship, to maintain personal and professional ties, and to move on from the bad news to accomplish something good another time, another place.

RELATED TOPICS

➤ **When Employees Discuss Sensitive Matters,** (pages 30–31)

➤ **When an Employee Is Caught in a Lie,** (pages 80–81)

Supervising and Managing Diverse Groups

You can't rush the results, but the process of demonstrating how to get along with others will gradually help team members recognize and even appreciate their differences. What's interesting is that—amid all the cultural, ethnic, and other background differences—people nearly always find similarities on which to build effective working relationships and come to realize that their differences actually expand the group's ability to solve problems and work effectively.

WORDS TO LIVE BY

"We love in others what we lack our-selves, and would be everything but what we are."
—Charles A. Stoddard

Although many people are afraid that diversity in the workplace requires supervisors and managers to turn a blind eye to problems, individual differences, and interpersonal conflicts, that's really just an expression of their fear of strangers—known in psychological terms as "xenophobia."

As an effective supervisor or manager, you can actually make diversity a positive force that improves the productivity and morale of the people working for you.

Here are a few suggestions to help you accomplish this:

1 Be a mirror for your team

Help everyone on your team improve their self-awareness by reflecting back to them their values, judgments, assumptions, and culturally induced behavior and beliefs. Do this not only with the minorities, but with everyone.

In fact, you might want to include a little self-awareness training or simple self-aware-ness experiences during some of your regular group meetings.

When people openly share information about their backgrounds, experiences, beliefs, and assumptions, they hear themselves in others and recognize the differences without having to label them "better" or "worse."

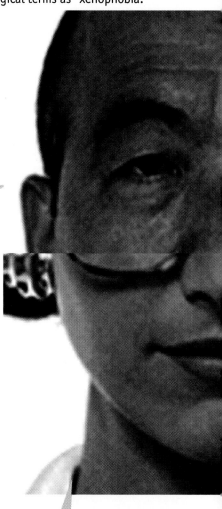

2 Demonstrate your sensitivity to others

Here's one way you can best lead by example. Work to develop relationships with people from diverse backgrounds. The employees you supervise or manage will sooner or later begin to follow your lead and do the same.

Notice that you needn't master or even understand all the nuances of the other person's culture and background. Simply begin to develop a relationship close enough that you're comfortable asking about whatever you need to know.

 **RED ALERT!**

Like most teams, yours probably has one person who is totally "clueless" about how to be sensitive to others. He or she can foment trouble without even knowing it. So pay extra attention to sensitizing this individual to his or her own mistaken beliefs and assumptions about coworkers who—on the surface—seem different.

3 Encourage those who can share

You've likely encountered people who show a "knee jerk" response of dislike and distrust for anyone who is "different." But you may not be aware that there are others with just as basic an instinct to establish relationships across lines of diversity.

As a supervisor or manager, you'll improve your team's results if you support and encourage these bridge-builders, instead of the bridge-destroyers.

4 Be slow to judge

One common source of interpersonal conflict results from simple misunderstandings. You see a person weeping and you automatically assume that he's weak. Later you learn that his wife is in the hospital undergoing a serious operation, and your opinion instantly changes.

Encourage all members of your work team to find out more about any seemingly different situation before they decide that another person is acting strangely or is not worthy of their respect and help.

 **RELATED TOPICS**

➤ **Building Team Spirit,** (pages 56–57)

➤ **Creative Problem Solving,** (pages 98–99)

Inside Info

One good exercise to help your team improve its spirit is to hold monthly "team improvement" sessions. Here, team members can point out to each other good opportunities to perform at a higher level. Encourage your team members to experiment with unusual ideas or approaches that seem to have potential value. Deciding on their own what to do and when not only improves productivity but also team spirit.

Building Team Spirit

Team spirit is hard to define, but it's easy to see and feel in action. Although team spirit tends to grow by itself, it takes a skilled supervisor or manager to nurture it and use it to enhance team productivity and success.

Here are some guidelines to help improve the spirit among the people who work for you:

1 Over time, select people who are right for the team, and transfer away or even let go people who tend to tear the team apart. Like a coach, you can't develop a winning team without having the right team members to put forward a coordinated, highly motivated effort toward an agreed-on goal.

2 Work to create a supportive environment for your team. Just collecting people in a group won't build team spirit unless the entire organization rewards cooperative, collaborative work methods, such as team-oriented performance evaluations.

3 Challenge your team to help the organization. Team spirit thrives in an atmosphere filled with short-term assignments, medium-term goals, and long-term missions linked directly to the organization's health and survival. When the team knows its work is important and valuable, each member tends to feel a stronger commitment level.

WORDS TO LIVE BY

"Never argue with people who buy ink by the gallon."
—Tommy Lasorda

4 Create a unique team identity. It takes more than a T-shirt, although that can certainly help. Teams with strong spirit and good productivity tend to hold common goals and values. They like to utilize the same methods of problem solving and decision making, and they know the importance of expressing their team's uniqueness to themselves and each other.

SKILL BUILDERS

Building Identity

Use the following strategies to support a unique team identity:

- Develop and promote a team motto or slogan that defines how the team operates
- Adopt a mascot
- Pursue a spirit-building activity
- Regularly elect a "team member of the week" (or the month) to honor a person's contributions to the team's special goals.

5 Encourage your team to use its initiative. Tackling problems and accepting assignments on its own initiative, reaching decisions and allocating resources according to its own best judgment, and taking chances or exploring new opportunities all boost a team's spirit level.

6 Make your team accountable. Part of taking responsibility for success is being willing to have your effort measured and evaluated. Team spirit increases when each member recognizes that his or her contribution is a vital part of the overall effort. Whether the team measures itself in terms of dollars, number of units, or even survey responses from customers, the mere process leads to growth of team spirit.

RELATED TOPICS

Empowering Your Employees, (pages 90–91)

Giving Team Members More Effective Roles to Play

ACTION — create → NEEDS — which satisfy → GOALS — achieve → ACTION

Part of supervising or managing a group of people, and forging them into a highly productive and satisfied team, is managing how they interact and relate to one another.

The key to success in this form of "team management" is to give each person their own special role to play within the overall team structure.

Although you should work with each individual to find and develop a unique role within which their skills and strengths are optimally utilized, there are four fundamental roles from which you should select elements in varying degrees to build a unique one for each team member. These four fundamental roles are:

The Strategist

No team can succeed without at least one person who sees the "big picture," who watches the far horizons for potential problems and opportunities, and who maintains a sense of direction toward important goals when everyone else is face down in the mud trying to move the team's wagon forward. This is strategy at its best.

There can be room on effective teams for more than one strategist, of course, provided they agree on an overall vision and cooperate rather than compete with each other to win the team's support for the directions they feel are most important to pursue.

The Networker

Some people seem to be born with a knack for human relations. They make everyone feel wanted, important, and central to the team's success. These people, often described as "networkers," have acquired or been blessed with the ability to recognize what other individuals want, need, and know, and they've learned the skill or been given the natural ability to bring others together into a cohesive unit.

Too many networkers on the same team can pose a problem—because they function as a kind of glue that keeps people working smoothly together, regardless of the pressures and forces tending to drive them apart.

 RED ALERT! Although every role type is important in a team situation, certain individuals may have more leadership ability and the inclination to take advantage of it. Don't let your team become a hierarchy with you as a lame duck. Diffuse any type of power situation when it first takes root and reinforce your message of teamwork.

The Dynamo

When work needs to be done—often long, hard, and thankless work—it's the "dynamo" who comes through for the team time and time again. This person is motivated by the challenge to complete specific, perhaps detailed tasks. He or she likes to be recognized as an expert and insists on the importance of doing quality work even against difficult obstacles.

The dynamo is normally a reliable, dependable force that habitually pushes the team closer to its goals, regardless of how demanding the circumstances.

The Rebel

Born to be wild, the "rebel" is actually a useful member of any dynamic, effective team. He or she is the catalyst for change, the individual with the unusual point of view, the person who asks the uncomfortable questions. The rebel on the team wants justifications for established procedures, basic assumptions, and even orders from "the boss." Although the rebel sometimes makes others nervous or uncomfortable, he or she makes up for the extra problems by driving the team to breakthrough levels of effectiveness.

RELATED TOPICS

➤ **Valuing Your Employees,** (pages 8–9)

➤ **Fighting Burnout,** (pages 72–73)

Handling the Problems of Downsizing

AT&T to cut 40,000 jobs; downsizing fears grip workers

Largest downsizing by an American company since IBM cut 63,00 jobs; GM once cut 50,000

By ABBY K.T. TIM

Employees of AT&T Corp. were wary yesterday after the nation's largest telecommunications company announced it would cut 40,000 jobs nationwide as part of a plan to break the company into three businesses.

"People are obviously concerned," said Randy Clooney, director of the AT&T research and development lab at Mont-

gomery Park in Willsburg. "We're all just hanging out, worrying and waiting."

Many local employees could be affected, from mail room workers to the highest ranking corporate officials.

Robert E. Allen, chairman of AT&T, said the job cuts announced yesterday are the most important part of the company's plan to divide into three independent businesses to remain competitive.

Please turn to AT&T, Page B12

As corporations continue to peel away layers of excess employees, the supervisors and managers who remain face the many problems of working with people who may have significant emotional and psychological problems.

Those employees who survive a round of corporate downsizing will frequently exhibit a measure of intellectual confusion, emotional fragility, and depression—with very disturbing consequences.

Often mistakenly diagnosed as "burnout"—the sudden loss of interest and motivation for the job—these problems require immediate and serious attention, or they can fester and grow much worse.

Symptoms

Keep on the lookout for any subtle but important shifts in your team members' perceptions and behavior. Monitor carefully for these symptoms:

Lack of motivation—An enthusiastic worker loses interest. A subordinate stops caring about your opinion. A person begins griping about everything. A solid worker suddenly takes on a "what's the point?" attitude.

Supernegativity—Workers seem to expect each day to be worse than the previous one. They predict unsatisfying results from every endeavor.

Lack of creativity—Employees no longer develop their own ideas and projects. They come to you for solutions to every problem. They ask for direction at every step.

Lateness and absenteeism—Employees who were once very punctual now miss appointments and working hours far too often.

Remedies

Restore trust, faith, and motivation. There's no panacea for everyone suffering from every form of "post downsizing" syndrome, but here are some proven possibilities:

Restore some certainty—Downsizing hurts because it's usually a sudden and seemingly random blow to situations people have believed to be stable. Your employees will bounce back to normal much faster if they feel some of that stability has been restored.

Do this by keeping job and team assignments steady, establishing clear work and training schedules, offering guaranteed minimum hours, and so forth. The more solid reference points you can provide, the better.

Make jobs positively exciting—The people you supervise or manage have had enough of the negative excitement for a while. It is now important for you to provide new challenges, interesting incentives, stronger motivations, and other "exciters" they'll look forward to.

Instead of coddling, some teams respond better to tougher assignments, challenging work opportunities, and whatever might give them hope for the future. By offering your team new training, chances to develop new procedures, or new equipment to work with, their attitudes may well swing back toward normal.

Be very aware of employees who begin to display dramatically different behavior. These individuals may not be dealing with their fear and stressful feelings about the eminent changes and may need some guidance from a professional.

RELATED TOPICS

➤ **Reducing Tardiness and Absenteeism, (pages 66–67)**

➤ **Fighting Burnout, (pages 72–73)**

➤ **Reducing Stress Levels, (pages 76–77)**

Maintaining Output with Minimal Staff

In many supervisory and management situations, maintaining a given level of output is vital. Doing so is easy when you're fully staffed, but sometimes open positions must go unfilled, or workers take sick days, vacation leave, and compensatory time just when you need them the most.

Maintaining Output

Here are some techniques for maintaining output levels under difficult staffing conditions.

1 Flexible scheduling

One of the advantages of some flexible scheduling schemes is that fewer people can produce more per day by working longer hours. Two of the most popular arrangements are four 10-hour days per week and—over a two-week period—nine 10-hour days. Both schemes provide a 25 percent boost in daily productivity from each person who comes to work.

2 Use temps

You can make up for being short-handed or for habitual understaffing by working with temps. An agency can find and send you properly skilled people as you need them, or you can manage your own pool of experienced people who are satisfied to work only at times of peak demand or to fill in when staff levels fall too low.

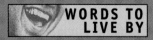

RED ALERT!

Don't allow routine, administrative, or intermittent responsibilities to take precedence over critically important tasks and thus drain scarce work hours. When staffing levels fall, let these concerns take a back seat until you have more people to put on them. If necessary, you can delegate these less important tasks to employees from other departments—or even use temps to handle them for you.

TimeSaver
Make a "short list" of each permanent employee's job description, briefly listing his or her chief responsibilities. When an employee goes on vacation or leaves the organization, you can then—at least temporarily—delegate these main responsibilities to others.

3 Create "assignment desks"

This is how newspapers, industrial analysts, and other organizations maintain levels of expertise and service regardless of staffing problems. To do this, you:

1 Define the most important "assignment desks," reflecting the critical processes that help determine the success (or failure) of the work for which you are responsible.

In a shipping department, for example, you might define "order picking," "packing," and "scheduling" desks. In a laboratory, your desks might be labeled "test scheduling," "test assigning," "testing," "result determination," and "report writing."

2 Each "assignment" can be physically located at a specific desk, stocked with the necessary resources and reference materials, or it can remain just a set of responsibilities that people work on wherever they happen to be.

3 Schedule hours when each of these "assignment desks" must be staffed. Then, as staffing levels change, you can redistribute these hours among your best available people.

When staff is scarce, you can keep the "desks" working by letting one person handle two or more different ones. This "desk" system lets you feel confident that critical assignments are never neglected for too long. Double and triple desk responsibilities may mean that work slows down, but it won't stop.

RELATED TOPICS

➤ Giving Team Members More Effective Roles to Play, (pages 58–59)

➤ Reducing Stress Levels, (pages 76-77)

Regular work groups usually produce tangible results that you can immediately notice and appreciate. Flexible and decentralized work groups, however, tend to temporarily disappear from view—except for what you assign them and for what they produce and deliver.

So concentrate your focus on these "deliverables." Keep track of what you're expecting, the current status of each one, and after delivery how well each completed item met your expectations and standards. This way your decentralized and flexible work group can become just as "alive" and "vivid" in your mind's eye as the people who sit in front of you every day of the week.

Handling Decentralized and Flexible Work Groups

With the increasing popularity of "flex time," "telecommuting," contractors, and other innovative approaches to employment, every supervisor and manager should master the skills needed to work effectively with decentralized and flexible work groups.

The key to success in these situations is to think a little farther ahead than you might be accustomed, and to act accordingly. For example:

1 *Schedule regular contacts.* With conventional work groups, you can call or visit on the spur of the moment—as each situation dictates. But decentralized and flexible work groups may not be available when you want to talk.

That's why supervisors and managers should learn to schedule a steady stream of contacts by telephone, E-mail, fax, video conference, or other channels.

Arrange the communication's starting time, ending time, and as much of an agenda as seems certain. But don't worry if you don't have much on the schedule for, say, next Tuesday. It's a sure bet some important matters will come up before then to more than fill that phone call.

2 *Make better use of meetings.* Because face-to-face meetings are relatively rare and difficult to arrange, effective supervisors and managers make them do double- and triple-duty.

Plan in some detail exactly what you'll cover at the meeting. Then prepare for those topics by doing the same level of research and analysis you'd do before a meeting with valued customers.

Plan carefully who should be in attendance. Include everyone who can contribute, so the meeting time counts for as much as possible.

Finally, consider where to hold the meeting. Your place? Their place? Some neutral site? A facility you want everyone to visit? Or perhaps a new territory you want everyone to investigate?

3 *Share information aggressively.* Your decentralized and flexible work group will be far more effective if its members have solid, regular access to the information they need. Since they can't just "pick it up" around the office, you'll have to shuttle it to them intentionally.

Consider all the various channels available to you: computer access points like the Internet or an electronic bulletin board, E-mail, postal mail, voice mail, fax-on-demand or other fax messaging systems, or perhaps even a newsletter you publish just to go over what decentralized and flexible employees may not find out on their own.

TO DO 1/14

Schedule group meeting for Friday 2:00 P.M.

Who to attend:
 entire tech support team; telecommuters, field & phone
 human resources contact—verify date & time with her

Need to contact:

Phone—
 Luce—in San Antonio today
 Renborn—traveling, leave message at NYC hotel
 Johanson—new computer installation today, probably off-line

E-mail
 Hiatt—jhiatt@walkon.com
 Thompson—rthompson@mirror.com

Broadcast fax (verify w/Angela to be sure everyone is covered)
 Rouf
 Toulouse
 Cohen
 tech support part-timers

Draft agenda—
Cover AccuTech contract _in detail_—(talk to Barb Roberts in Legal tomorrow!)
 why negotiations changed—leave no gray areas/explain the delays
 terms of service—who does what
 expectations re: telecommuters and their responsibilities
Outline new benefits package
 explain terminology re: "menu options"
 introduce human resources contact
 verify insurance co. contacts for future questions

Call MIS
 discuss possibilities of adapting Web page for internal use
 can we a get specific pages password-protected?
 use for internal communication only
 advocate for dedicated SYSOP for our BBS
 no more sharing with Sales!

RELATED TOPICS

▶ **Running Better Meetings,** (pages 22–23)

▶ **Juggling Multiple Priorities** (pages 24–25)

You'll probably notice the 80-20 rule operating here: 20 percent of the employees chalk up 80 percent of the lateness and absences. Also, 20 percent of their excuses cover 80 percent of their missed hours and days.

If you closely focus your remedial work on these 20 percenters, you'll find you can more easily put a lid on your team's overall lateness and absence figures.

WORDS TO LIVE BY

"Some people are always late, like the late King George V."

—Spike Milligan

Reducing Tardiness and Absenteeism

There's an undeniable tendency for people to stretch a weekend, enjoy the first day of the hunting season, stay home to watch a ball game, and so forth. But you can minimize absenteeism and lateness—including "opportunistic" offenders—by enlisting your team in the effort.

Consider taking some or all of the following steps:

Identify the Worst Offenders

It's easy to lose track of who's late or absent if you don't maintain accurate records. One good way is to log each lateness and absence on a monthly calendar. Mark down the offender's initials, or use a different color ink for each team member.

Spot the Patterns

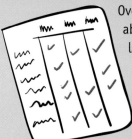 Over a period of months and years, this log of absences will reveal the underlying patterns of lateness and absence. You'll begin to see who is chronically late or absent, how often, and on what days. This will help you understand when and where absenteeism generally strikes.

It will also show you if certain days of the week or month aren't covered adequately or if the team is generally undermotivated about reliably showing up for work.

Attack the Problem Areas

It's your call as to whether a particular problem requires individual or team attention. Some patterns are best handled one on one—for example, a team member who regularly adds a day off to gain 3-day weekends, misses the same day of the month more often than would be coincidental, or always takes off for the start of hunting season or the first sunny day of spring.

Some problems, however, run through the entire team. For example, absences might pile up on the exact days your team counts inventory, attends refresher training, or does other unpopular workplace chores.

Involve Your Team Members

Discuss the lateness and absence problems—without naming individuals—in your team meetings. Post the statistics in your memos or on your bulletin board. You can even list "excessive lateness and absences" as one of your team's high-priority problems to solve.

Once you win their cooperation, your team members can help you uncover reasons for the problem and find cost-effective solutions.

TimeSaver
A quick way to reduce lateness is to offer bonus days off for employees who have been on time and not absent for a period of time.

Establish an Anti-absence Program

Whether you make it a formal program or an informal effort, you reduce absences the most when you work at this goal over the long haul. Some useful steps might be to:

• Post the absence figures each week or month and then use the data to make a graph indicating whether absences are trending up or down within your team.

• Reserve some bonus money or develop another worthwhile reward—perhaps a catered lunch or attractive team T-shirts—to use as a carrot that's delivered only when absences reach a certain (lower) level.

RED ALERT!

You can't do anything about lateness or absenteeism until you've posted and explained your organization's absenteeism policy and reviewed the consequences of repeated violations with all the members of your team. Only after you have laid out the policy and the expectations can you move on to individual counseling, remotivating, and occasionally disciplining repeat offenders.

RELATED TOPICS

➤ Giving Effective Feedback, (pages 46–47)
➤ Distributing Non-monetary Rewards, (pages 50–51)

The most effective motivational programs tend to be:

- *Achievable*—set your standards so everyone can meet them, not just the few best

- *Objective*—make clear what each person must do to succeed

- *Rewarding*—select prizes or payoffs that will actually motivate your team members

- *Timely*—the longer you wait to deliver a reward for good work, the less impact it carries

- *Useful*—measure and reward something important to producing useful results

WORDS TO LIVE BY

"The nail that sticks up gets hammered down."

—Japanese proverb

Motivation as a Daily Part of the Job

With today's propensity toward flexible work schedules, part-timers, temps, independent contractors, work sharing, and other nonconventional arrangements, it's become more difficult for time-honored supervisory techniques—raises, promotions, favorable written evaluations, and so forth—to work their motivational magic.

Instead, successful supervisors and managers are learning to use more personal, innovative ways to maintain and increase motivation as a daily part of doing the job. Here are some techniques to help you:

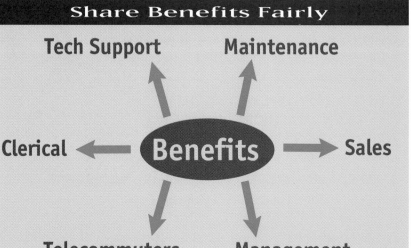

Share Benefits Fairly

Tech Support   Maintenance

Clerical ← **Benefits** → Sales

Telecommuters   Management

Every member who keeps the team productive deserves a fair share of the interesting new assignments, career development opportunities, honors, awards, pictures on the wall, favored parking places, or other motivational goodies you hand out. Even though you may not see them regularly, be sure to include such important members of your team as the telecommuting typists and the contract maintenance personnel who work after hours to keep things running smoothly.

Before you decide who should receive the choice benefits, go over the complete lists of everyone you might consider for each opportunity. It's even better if you can keep their names individually "alive" in your mind. One way to do so is by talking with each team member regularly about future plans. Another is by working with them whenever possible to upgrade their skills or increase their knowledge so that they're better qualified for upcoming opportunities.

Be as Flexible as Possible

Many people enjoy doing difficult or demanding work, or covering what others think are inconvenient hours. Some people are even willing to do the grunt work simply because they want to help you and the rest of the organization succeed.

WORK

- **Child care**
- **Remodeling project**
- **Auto accident**
- **Sick parent**
- **Moving**
- **School functions**

Keep these dedicated employees highly motivated by trying hard to accom-modate any reasonable requests they may make for, say, a few days off for child care or time off for other personal reasons.

Motivate Technical Specialists

"I need . . ."

"I can supply . . ."

"The problem is . . ."

"I am concerned . . ."

Unlike employees with more generalized skills, technical specialists generally have a passion for their work. That's why they can stay extremely motivated all by themselves and are often labeled "self-starters." Frequently, however, these specialists become so wrapped up in technical issues that they lose interest in anything else.

When this happens, they'll rarely respond positively to a supervisor or manager trying to change their behavior unless they feel some rapport and mutual respect. To develop this necessary communication, try using your influence to obtain the resources they want and need to work more effectively. You may also win their respect by listening as they discuss triumphs and tragedies in their respective area of technical expertise.

RED ALERT!

Don't be forced into denying your most critical workers' requests for temporary schedule changes because you have no one else to work the needed hours. Instead, keep your team's productivity and motivational levels high by grooming others to play "back up" for difficult or inconvenient assignments.

Ask for volunteers who want to help their teammates have a better chance for needed relief from difficult assignments, and then train these volunteers to handle the critical jobs.

TimeSaver

An occasional day away from the office, to discuss teamwork in the greater sense, often has an invigorating and motivational result. For organizations that heavily rely on teamwork, weekend "bonding" retreats can inspire new levels of commitment from team members.

RELATED TOPICS

➤ **Effective Training Practices,** (pages 74–75)

Be prepared. One day your mentor will have little else to tell you. When that happens, it's time to step up to a newer, better mentor. The following signs may be an indication that you've outgrown your mentor:

• You no longer ask for advice, only confirmation of what you know.

• You feel stifled or uncomfortable with your mentor.

• You must exaggerate your actual level of enthusiasm for your mentor's ideas and information.

WORDS TO LIVE BY

"It's what you learn after you know it all that counts."

—John Wooden

The Advantages of Mentoring

The term *mentor* comes from Greek legends, which report that Ulysses' son Telemachus learned his most significant lessons about living and ruling a kingdom from his very wise and experienced teacher, Mentor. Since then, thousands of people have shared their experience and knowledge with others—often to the mutual advantage of both. The best mentors are willing to be a combination coach, confidante, sounding board, and counselor. In return, they expect the "mentee" to work hard, to be worthy of all this attention, and to provide the mentor with whatever helpful information and feedback he or she can.

A mentor offers a "safe harbor" where it's OK to ask naive questions and even to make uninformed suggestions or offer incomplete ideas and plans. A mentor—like a parent—points out mistakes without judging and offers advice and guidance in solving difficult problems or assessing complex situations—ranging from technical expertise to social intelligence, career development, and corporate culture.

Today, many hundreds of organizations recognize the importance and value of mentoring and encourage their youngest and oldest executives to pair up for the transfer of experience, information, and overall business savvy.

If you're already successful, you might consider becoming a mentor to someone else, or, if you want to expand your career, try finding a mentor of your own. In general, mentors find it very rewarding to offer information, insight, and advice that helps another person blossom and fulfill his or her potential.

From either side, here's the best way to develop a solid mentor-mentee relationship:

Start Now

Mentoring is so helpful that it's never too late to begin. The sooner you start, the more advantages you gain. In fact, it's better to mentor (or be mentored by) a peer you trust and respect than not to enter into a mentoring relationship at all.

Try not to force a mentoring situation that doesn't work. Even though your work backgrounds and goals are similar, you may be paired up with someone you simply don't get along with. If so, graciously approach the other person and speak to them about dissolving the partnership with no hard feelings.

RED ALERT!

Screen for Someone You Like

Mentoring is based on very personal, selective determinations. It's usually more beneficial to pair with someone whose knowledge and experience differ substantially from your own. However, if mutual trust and commitment are lacking, the mentoring experience will not progress very far.

Have an Agenda

From either position, that is, the mentor or the mentee, be clear about what you're giving and getting in the relationship. Know your personal and career goals, and tap the other person for any information, expertise, or personal understanding that can bring you closer to your goals.

Don't Confuse the Process

Although mentoring involves close personal interaction, it is *not* a love affair, or even a close friendship. Rather, it's a contract for mutual aid and support. Although mentoring often leads to strong attachments, it can also result in territorial disputes and distrust. A mentor relationship will succeed only when both sides are firmly focused on professional issues.

RELATED TOPICS

➤ Setting Goals, (pages 26–27)

➤ Effective Training Practices, (pages 74–75)

Even with the best intentions, sometimes you simply burn out. Learn to recognize the signs of burnout and take the appropriate measures to recuperate and rejuvenate your body and mind.

Fighting Burnout

There are many possible reasons for "burnout"—the sudden loss of enthusiasm, interest, and motivation for the job. Burnout can strike after people work too hard for too long, push themselves or let themselves be pushed toward unreachable goals, or suffer problems and reversals in their personal lives that bleed over into the workplace.

Unchecked and untreated, burnout can eventually lead to the same kind of intellectual confusion, emotional fragility, and depression associated with people suffering "post-traumatic stress syndrome" after wars, earthquakes, hurricanes, and other hyperdangerous situations.

If you suspect a burnout problem among your team members, don't wait for orders from above. Here's how to proceed:

Look for Burnout Causes

Like a plumbing leak, burnout will nearly always continue to cause problems and even get worse until you find and eliminate the source. Consider whether any of these factors might be unduly influencing your team:

1 Disappointment
When a person's expectations or hopes are unceremoniously shattered, burnout can result. While this may not happen the first ten times, the more frequently you experience disappointment, the more likely you'll have a bout of burnout.

2 Uncertainty
Today the typical workplace is less certain than ever. This creates situations where people simply run out of tolerance for ambiguity, shades of gray, and impending changes they can't predict.

3 Anxiety
Many people cannot withstand the kind of pressure they now face to perform accurately, speedily, and responsively in today's workplace. They cope temporarily in a state of anxiety and then experience burnout.

 RED ALERT!

Symptoms of burnout often manifest when a person decides to start looking for other work. And although this lackluster behavior looks like a classic case of burnout, you needn't lose this employee. If he or she has performed well in the past, you can resurrect previous enthusiasm with the proper combination of individual counseling, training, and remotivation that—in effect—remakes the old job into an enjoyable "new" one.

Look for Remedies

Fighting burnout requires deliberate action over the long term. Here are two positive strategies to remedy this nonproductive emotional state:

1 Look to the future
Some burnout results from boredom or lack of direction. Rejuvenate these sufferers by offering new challenges, incentives, training, and other motivators. Sometimes, tougher rather than easier assignments are the best remedy.

2 Share the feelings
Burnout is often a reaction from being overwhelmed by on-the-job events. You probably can't undo what's done, but you can offer a sympathetic ear and a supportive attitude that will help your people recover as quickly as possible.

 **RELATED TOPICS**

➤ Reducing Stress Levels, (pages 76–77)

➤ Managing Workplace Anger, (pages 84–85)

Inside Info

Basically, you will want to organize training in three levels:

1. The first and most basic level covers the gaps in fundamental job-related knowledge your team members ought to know, but don't.

2. The intermediate level of training covers advanced skills and broader understanding that will enable your already successful team members to do an even better job.

3. The third level of training builds on the first two and is aimed at enhancing your team members, leadership, creative problem-solving, and self-management skills so they can function more independently and contribute more to the organization's overall productivity.

WORDS TO LIVE BY

"Act the way you'd like to be and soon you'll be the way you act."
—**Dr. George W. Crane**

Effective Training Practices

Most supervisors and managers understand that training is one of the best methods for teaching employees new skills, procedures, work methods, and technology. But it takes many years before some recognize the additional value of training as a subtle but effective way to spread experience and work ethic among team members, as well as to build loyalty and motivation.

Generally, you want training done by experts who understand both the subject matter and the best way to convey it. Keep in mind, however, that there are situations where training experts have less impact than others. For example, when your organization or team uses extremely individualized procedures, the best trainer might be someone who uses them on a daily basis.

In addition, there are situations when the best way to train an employee is to meld conventional training with daily work assignments, creating an atmosphere that mixes learning and doing. This benefits both "teachers" and "students" by providing opportunities to work with and learn from coworkers who can share their special skills and experience.

In "buddy system" training, for example, you pair off people and let them know they'll be working together a good portion of their time during the next several weeks, months, or even longer.

From then on, you make assignments to the pair, not the separate individuals. Ideally, you'll find ways to give both members of the "buddy" team enough demanding work to keep them both busy. If you handle it correctly, you'll get higher quality results from the less-skilled one of the buddies than you would normally expect. At the same time, you'll also get more top-flight production from the most-skilled buddy than he or she would normally produce when working alone.

To make the buddy system more effective, evaluate both members of the team not only on the usual factors such as productivity and quality but also on the level of buddy improvement they show as a team. Such a focus will help ensure that the training aspects of their assignments will be perceived as an integral part of their workdays.

If you can't pair up certain members of your team, you can get almost the same results by using certain assignments as training tools. For example, you probably have projects—like designing new forms for internal use—where small mistakes or slight delays are relatively harmless. Use these to train up-and-coming employees. Assign each of them the projects you feel will demand their best efforts.

Don't intimidate people into a "sink or swim" situation. Ask your more knowledgeable and experienced people to be ready to help whenever needed. Make clear that there's no penalty for requesting help. In fact, learning where to get assistance can become an important part of the training value of the assignment.

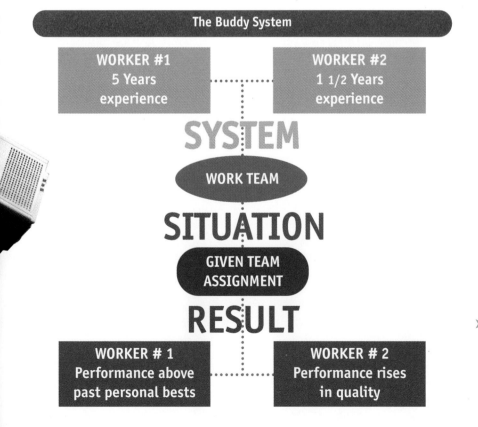

The Buddy System

WORKER #1 — 5 Years experience

WORKER #2 — 1 1/2 Years experience

SYSTEM — WORK TEAM

SITUATION — GIVEN TEAM ASSIGNMENT

RESULT

WORKER #1 Performance above past personal bests

WORKER #2 Performance rises in quality

RELATED TOPICS

➤ Giving Team Members More Effective Roles to Play, (pages 58–59)

Inside Info

It's relaxing to switch between different types of work as you feel tension mounting. Change the muscle groups you're using, the senses you're overstimulating, even your body position—from sitting to standing, or standing to squatting. Variety is not only the spice of life but also a "relaxation tonic" on the job.

Reducing Stress Levels

Many supervisors and managers mistakenly attribute overwork and demanding pressures on the job as reasons for their feelings of stress. In reality, however, it's not their work that's causing stress, it's their *reaction* to their work! And while you can't change much about what goes on at your workplace, you *can* dramatically change how you react to it. That's the secret of reducing your stress level.

Here are some proven techniques to reduce stress on the job:

Change your attitude

There's forest, and there's trees. Paying too much attention to one can easily raise your stress level. Focusing a little more often on the other can lower it.

It's OK, of course, to concentrate on the trees—the tasks you need to complete—as you work hour to hour. You're probably very good at that. But learn to take time at least twice a day to look at the entire forest. In what direction are you headed?

How much progress have you made? What opportunities and difficulties lay ahead? Refocusing your eyes from the trees to the whole forest immediately reduces your concentration on the unending pressures to perform and the complex details you must master. It also allows you to consciously decide where to put your best efforts next time you start clearing out the trees.

Cultivate a "calm scene"

One good way to instantly produce relaxation anywhere you happen to be is to develop your own private "calm scene." Visualize yourself out in nature or in a Las Vegas casino—wherever you feel most comfortable. If you don't like one scene, create another.

Then keep practicing your concentration on this calm scene each time you take a break. After a while, you'll be able to relax in a few seconds, and get the equivalent of hours of "decompression" in just a few minutes.

WORDS TO LIVE BY

"Stress kills."
—**Anonymous**

Give yourself time to recover

Pressure takes its toll. Like carrying a heavy boulder, it bends you and tires you and makes work seem extremely burdensome. But as soon as you put it down, you feel much lighter.

That's why it's important to commit to a little relaxation, recuperation, and enjoyment time every day. After work hours, become involved in a hobby or pastime. Even during work hours, take five-minute breaks a few times a day when you can walk, breathe deeply, and simply relax in private.

RED ALERT! Caffeine, which is in coffee, teas, many soft drinks, and even some over-the-counter cold and headache remedies, can contribute to and increase stress levels.

TimeSaver
Practice stress-relief measures *before* you need them. Learn about relaxation exercises such as yoga and meditation or find a personal way of quietly reducing stress levels.

RELATED TOPICS

➤ Supervising and Managing Diverse Groups, (pages 54–55)

➤ Resolving Conflicts Effectively, (pages 88–89)

Inside Info

You can rein in your rebels by avoiding general arguments over their personalities or attitudes. Instead, itemize each rule violation—date, time, place, circumstances—and ask for explanations. Listen carefully for why they broke the rule. You may find clues to help prevent further problems.

Remember that the "rebel" is an important force in successful teams—asking the tough questions and demanding good reasons for every action and decision. View the rebels on your team not as terrorist destroyers but as confrontive supporters of the team's agreed-on goals and objectives.

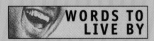

WORDS TO LIVE BY

"They sicken of the calm, who know the storm."

—Dorothy Parker

Handling Rebellious or Negative Employees

It's not only difficult but also unproductive to have employees who work against you. You don't want anyone to rebel against your authority—regardless of the validity or invalidity of their reason. Nor do you want people to indiscriminately say "no" or "what's the use?" to every suggestion, idea, possibility, or opportunity crossing their path.

Such rebels and nay-sayers can easily destroy the morale, productivity, and interlinked relationships of your team, as well as trash some highly interesting opportunities. So it's important that you take a strong stand to make things more positive as soon as you recognize what you're dealing with. Here are some proven ways to handle the following "personas" displayed by rebellious or negative employees:

Limit the Controller

Some people use consistent negativity to control situations. Driven by fear of failure, they try to keep items off the agenda, limit others' options, and occasionally just shout down the opposition.

The best response is to help the "negative controller" learn to limit his or her risk in other ways. Thoughtful planning and taking smaller steps are often useful. Sometimes, controllers can learn to be comfortable with slightly more risk, particularly when the risk is balanced by highly attractive rewards.

Harness the Solo Achiever

People who insist on working alone when they shouldn't often create problems for everyone else who is supposed to be on their team.

Integrate their energy and efforts into the team a little better by pairing the solo operator with someone who has complementary skills. Then assign them work that neither one can accomplish alone.

Disarm the Backstabber

These are people who use sabotage and backstabbing to achieve success by keeping others from doing well. Assuming you've inadvertently hired or inherited one of these people on your team, the best response is "zero tolerance"—that is, don't listen to their criticisms of others, don't act on what they tell you about others, and don't let them have their way.

TimeSaver
Offer periodic reminders to all employees of what behavior is unacceptable. A good way to do this is by conducting periodic company-wide seminars of your organization's policies. By doing this, you can reinforce good behavior while also reminding those renegade employees that bad behavior will *not* be tolerated.

Rehabilitate the Frequent Victim

Some people are bound for disaster, while others just enjoy putting a negative spin on every new development and often claim they have no power to control the events that occur "around them."

Your best response here is to focus on future opportunities. Offer them training and challenges. Help them to actualize their potential. Each triumph tends to remove some weight from this person's burden. If not, at least it gives you ammunition to disagree next time he or she complains about being a victim.

Re-educate the Negative Expert

If a person wants to badly enough, he or she can find a dozen reasons why any plan won't work and any job can't be done. They've become a negative expert.

With time and energy, however, you can change their analysis. Start by that insisting he or she be very specific in every criticism. This gives you a basis to strengthen plans that are weak and then devote more resources toward difficult tasks. After he or she achieves positive results, it's much more difficult to maintain a negative stance.

RELATED TOPICS

➤ When an Employee Is Caught In a Lie, (pages 80–81)

➤ Taming the Bully, (pages 82–83)

➤ Managing Workplace Anger, (pages 84–85)

Inside Info

When the situation boils down to one employee's word against another's, stop thinking in terms of blatant "truth" and "lies." Instead, handle the controversy as a dispute to be resolved.

When an Employee Is Caught in a Lie

Most people on your team are probably honest and truthful. But, under the right circumstances, almost everyone can be induced to tell a "little white lie." And sometimes the lies are bigger and darker.

In past situations, you've probably felt fairly comfortable dealing with employees who have made a single exaggeration, falsification, or omission of selected facts from a story, and such a minor infraction likely resulted in a reprimand, not an immediate dismissal.

But when you encounter a regular, consistent pattern of unreliable reporting, telling tall tales, or recasting the facts to suit the moment's agenda, you may not be so comfortable about what actions to take. Here are some guidelines to help you:

Ascertain the undisputed facts

Confront in private

It's a major mistake to accuse people of lying when you're not sure of the exact circumstances. So before you say a word about—or even hint at—your suspicions, research the events in question and nail down as many of the facts as you can.

It's rarely—if ever—a wise idea to launder your team's dirty linen in public. Instead, select a nice, quiet place where you can confront the suspected liar in private.

PRIVATE

WORDS TO LIVE BY

"The truth is the safest lie."

—Anonymous

Reveal what you know

You're trying to sandbag the liar—or play Nancy Drew—when you ask about the situation and try to catch the suspected offender in a lie. Don't bother. Straightforwardly and as calmly as possible state what you absolutely know to be true. Produce any evidence you have discovered. Then request an explanation.

Evaluate the response

It takes a hardened liar to keep up a pretense when faced with cold, hard facts. When that's the response, begin documenting both the employee's behavior and your warnings. You'll probably wind up terminating this person, and a strong written record will make that action more bullet-proof.

Most times, however, the employee will admit the lie and offer a reason for it. You can then evaluate the reasonableness of that story—and the motivation behind it.

Punish fairly

When you've caught an employee lying for the first time, you may want to provide no more punishment than an oral warning. In more severe cases, you may choose to switch the liar to a different job or a lower authority level.

When you notice that lying has become repetitive, however, that's a long step down the road to termination. So provide a written warning for their permanent personnel file.

RELATED TOPICS

➤ Creative Problem Solving, (pages 98–99)

You won't convert bullies overnight. Having spent most of their lives defeating fear through bullying behavior, they haven't developed too many other reactions. But steadfastly refuse to let bullying work for them, and hold out the promise of better results from more socially accepted behavior. Under this double whammy, even the toughest bully will feel the urge to find new ways of relating to others.

Taming the Bully

It's an unfortunate tendency, but some people in the workplace will seek out or even manufacture opportunities to put physical, mental, or emotional pressure on people who are smaller, younger, or weaker than themselves.

Most often, one person may want another to take the blame for a mistake, to do favors, or to assume responsibility for the least enjoyable work tasks. But there can be as many scenarios for bullying as there are grains of sand on the beach.

Here are some practical approaches to fight bullying in the work group you supervise or manage:

Recognize the Bully

Whether or not you've ever been personally bullied, you probably know that bullies use threats to influence others' behavior. Actually, most bullies are ordinary people who simply don't recognize when they go too far.

Regardless of the nature of the bullying pattern, you can be sure most bullying behavior is motivated mainly by fear. When the bully feels afraid—whatever the reason or situation—he or she tries to control that fear by making others even more fearful. Bullies tend to concentrate on people who won't fight back, and they're rarely satisfied with occasional bullying. When they find someone to intimidate, they like to make it a regular and relentless pattern.

Block the Bully

A possible supervisory tactic would be to attempt to help the bully overcome his or her fear in hopes of eliminating bullying behavior. But other employees would likely suffer while you're focusing excessive attention on the bully—and, of course, there's no guaranteed success that his or her behavior will change for the better.

There's also a temptation to bully back, trying to overpower the bully by mirroring his very own tactics. This almost never works. Bullies enjoy the use of power, so your pressure will generally do nothing but motivate them to bully even more in other situations.

It's more practical, therefore, to simply prevent the bully from doing harm to others. The best initial strategy is to prevent bullies from getting good results this harmful way and then to prove that there are more effective ways to reduce their underlying fears.

"I have always believed, and I still believe, that whatever good or bad fortune may come our way we can always give it meaning and transform it into something of value."

—Hermann Hesse

These three simple steps will help you eliminate most bullying behavior in the shortest possible time:

1 Maintain a detached attitude. The more you "care" about the threats and counterthreats involved in the bullying, the more you're playing into the bully's hands.

2 Talk about what the bully is doing. Don't yell or argue. Focus on the behavior instead of the person, with the attitude that "bullying will *not* get you what you want."

3 Wait an hour, a day, or even a week—until the bully is less fearful. Then have a private chat, and discuss alternatives to such undesirable behavior.

RED ALERT! Many supervisors and managers make the mistake of thinking it's their responsibility to "diagnose" the bully's problem and then help him or her "cure" it. Such psychoanalysis is well beyond the scope of their duties. Instead, just focus on how to stop the bullying behavior.

CASE IN POINT

As a new supervisor in Organic Garments' mail-order department, Ross Donaldson found himself facing down Julie Handey on a daily basis. First she was bullying the customers, so Ross took her off the phone lines. Then, she began intimidating her coworkers, vying for a better workstation. Faced with the challenge of resolving the issue or transferring Julie to another department, Ross did the following:

1. He began watching her closely, and let her know that she was being monitored. This made Julie more aware of her behavior, and she immediately began bullying her coworkers less.

2. When Julie did get her way with one of the other employees, Ross stepped in without hesitation and overrode the decision. By indicating that bullying was not going to get her what she wanted, Ross again reinforced positive over negative behavior.

3. On the occasions when Julie handled a stressful situation well and without intimidation, Ross praised her publicly.

RESOLVE OR TRANSFER?

- Monitor the bully
- Let the bully know he's being monitored
- Step in as necessary
- Give praise when appropriate

EVALUATE THE RESULT

RELATED TOPICS

➤ Handling Rebellious or Negative Employees, (pages 78–79)

An angry scene rarely stands alone. It's usually the result of forces that have been festering within individuals over a long period of time. Help these angry people get back to a more comfortable emotional level by counseling them to take constructive steps to change the forces that have contributed to this negative emotion. If that's not possible, at least encourage them to "work off" their anger through sports, creativity, or a hobby.

WORDS TO LIVE BY

"I am a kind of paranoiac in reverse. I suspect people of plotting to make me happy."

—J. D. Salinger

Managing Workplace Anger

Just because people spend time in the workplace doesn't mean they check their emotions at the door. And one of the strongest emotions is anger.

People feel and express their anger at many different levels and for many different reasons. We all experience occasional temper tantrums, but normally the storm passes and we calm back down. But here we're talking about more serious anger. If you want to be a successful supervisor or manager, you must learn not only how to deal with certain types and levels of anger but also how to recognize the "hot potatoes" you dare not touch.

Here are some basic guidelines for dealing with angry employees under your authority:

Remove the Cause

Anger is nearly always a reaction. To manage this emotion, you should try to learn specifically what *triggered* the reaction. If it's under your control, you may be able to reduce the stimulation to anger. If it's beyond your control, it's still possible for you to help the individual channel his anger into something more constructive.

Although extreme anger rarely builds in a single afternoon, a long-simmering level of emotion can be set off by something simple: an isolated yet uncomfortable experience, a conflict with a coworker, a seemingly innocent remark, or even a subtle threat to the angry person's status or position within the team.

You can often help put a lid on the employee's anger simply by removing whatever triggered it. If it's a person, send him or her away for a while. If it's a problem confrontation, immediately extricate the angry person from the environment.

Although you can't "unring" a bell or "unsay" a remark that prompted the anger, you can usually veer the subject toward something that will capture the angry person's interest enough to shift the triggering remark into the background.

Protect the Innocent

You have to protect yourself and your team members from harm—whether the anger manifests verbally or physically.

Look for ways to isolate the angry person from co-workers. For example, order everyone else out of the room. Take the angry person outside, or call for a private meeting in a room where others can't see or hear what's going on.

In extreme cases, it's also important to look for ways to render the angry person less dangerous. Shut down any machinery, for example, and hide or get rid of any scissors, knives, and noxious chemicals.

RED ALERT! The biggest danger is that an angry person will lose control and harm himself or others. When anger erupts, keep an eye peeled for any tools, implements, raw materials, or even weapons that can turn a temper tantrum into a tragedy. If you spot one, decide whether you can safely remove it from the scene. If you can't, the situation is much more ticklish, and you should consider calling for help—either higher authority or physical security—at your earliest opportunity.

Don't Overpower

Don't play the "John Wayne" role and try to overpower the angry person. It's far better to let him or her express this anger—safely—as a means of lowering the emotional temperature and calming the angry scene.

When anger threatens to escalate into violence, call for security personnel.

Offer a Time-out

Employees who express too much anger too openly at work are usually embarrassed and uncomfortable afterward. It can be very difficult for them to return to work as though nothing had happened.

For this reason, it's wise for you to provide an optional time-out by offering them a chance to take off the rest of the day or, in extreme cases, the rest of the week.

RELATED TOPICS

➤ Handling Violence in the Workplace, (pages 44–45)

➤ Giving Effective Feedback, (pages 46–47)

Most organizations establish dress-down days on Fridays. But this compounds the problem of employees feeling work can slip a little that day, because it's the last day of the work week. Sometimes, it's better to put casual-dress days at the start of the week, when people normally feel more incentive to get projects started and to wrap up work accumulated during the weekend.

Managing Casual-dress Days

Monday   Tuesday   Wednesday   Thursday   Friday

According to CNBC television network news, about 85 million workers in the United States presently enjoy at least one "dress-down" day per week, and more are expected to join them as the trend sweeps irresistibly through more and more workplaces.

Although most people feel casual-dress days are more convenient, comfortable, and even fun, some supervisors and managers worry that the withdrawal of time-tested dress codes can do more harm than good.

Here are some techniques, however, that can help you keep job performance high on dress-down days:

Establish Minimum Dress Codes

It's OK to dress more comfortably at work, but it may not be acceptable for people to come to work in your area wearing flip-flops, miniskirts, tank tops, cutoffs, or other forms of casual wear. If you have customers or visitors frequently walking through your job site, such attire will be even more disruptive, making it easy for them to feel your team has lost its professionalism.

The solution is to compromise between regular work attire and beachwear. Simple dress-down standards can require, for example, some form of sleeves on all tops, mid-thigh or longer shorts and skirts, and quiet (non-flapping) shoes. All this lends a general air of "informal professionalism" without destroying the benefits of dress-down days.

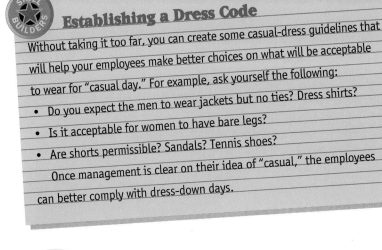

Establishing a Dress Code

Without taking it too far, you can create some casual-dress guidelines that will help your employees make better choices on what will be acceptable to wear for "casual day." For example, ask yourself the following:

- Do you expect the men to wear jackets but no ties? Dress shirts?
- Is it acceptable for women to have bare legs?
- Are shorts permissible? Sandals? Tennis shoes?

Once management is clear on their idea of "casual," the employees can better comply with dress-down days.

RED ALERT!

Nearly everyone who participates in dress-down days at work enjoys them. But don't be seduced by the informal clothing into thinking that quality standards, productivity standards, and overall results can be compromised as well.

You may have to exert a little more direction on casual-dress days, or at least caution your team about the tendency to relax performance standards along with the more casual dress codes. Be alert to the problem, and do what you must to ensure that dress-down days don't harm the organization's overall level of success.

Compare Productivity

Most organizations establish dress-down days to ease the pressure, cost, and discomfort of wearing dresses, suits, and similar outfits at work. In fact, in some situations the relaxed dress codes have sparked a modest *increase* in output.

In any case, productivity certainly shouldn't follow dress codes downward. It's a good idea to keep records and compare productivity on dress-up and dress-down days. Look at such factors as tardiness in the morning and after lunch, early departures, and the volume of work completed per hour. Also be alert on casual-dress days for such tendencies as not finishing tasks, and not starting new ones, either.

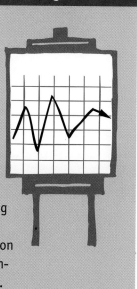

RELATED TOPICS

> **Building Team Spirit, (pages 56–57)**

Resolving Conflicts Effectively

Inside Info

Conflicts can be very difficult for supervisors and managers to resolve satisfactorily primarily because they often fall into a gray area where managerial authority is unclear or the disputes are so complex that there is no single, "right" resolution.

Your best strategy is to de-emphasize the "rightness" or "wrongness" of the conflict and focus instead on limiting damage to the organization, your team, the individuals on it, as well as your overall mission or work objectives.

Any time you have two or more people together, you will eventually have conflicts. Disagreements and infighting can occur over responsibilities and extra authority as well as over "blame" for past mistakes. You may also encounter personal jealousies and other forms of emotional conflict.

As supervisor or manager, it's an important part of your job to keep these conflicts to a minimum. You'll also need to provide damage control and

The Ally

In this role, you deliberately side with one party to the conflict and work toward a resolution that favors his or her interests. But pick your conflicts carefully—playing The Ally almost inevitably creates tension between you and those you oppose.

The Ally's Tactics: Lend your moral and emotional support, help devise actions and monitor reactions, and use your personal and organizational authority, including your contacts and credibility.

The Advocate

To play The Advocate, focus on helping one side get what it wants as quickly and easily as possible.

It's best to play The Advocate when a conflict has little to do with your department or work group. As The Advocate, you can remain scrupulously fair.

The Advocate's Tactics: The Advocate and The Ally use many of the same tools to get their side a "win." But The Advocate presumably possesses a little more objectivity regarding the conflict.

WORDS TO LIVE BY

"Peace is the skillful management of conflict."
—Kenneth Boulding

relationship repair whenever possible after the conflict has been resolved, so that the team continues to function smoothly and effectively.

The simplest method of conflict resolution is to get and keep all parties "reasoning together." But this course of action is not always feasible. It may then become necessary for you to assume the most appropriate role to help patch up or even eliminate the particular conflict.

Review on this page and the previous one the four main roles and the accompanying tactics you can learn to use to resolve those more difficult conflicts:

The Moderator

In this role, you use your prestige and impartiality to help the disputants "reason together" and to encourage good faith negotiation and compromise. Again, you shouldn't be in a position to gain from either side's victory.

This role works best during high-profile conflicts that are separate from the interests of your work group or department, or for some conflicts entirely within your group.

The Moderator's Tactics: Maintain a level playing field, and fight for fairness on all sides. Use argument, persuasion, and power (where appropriate) to keep all sides communicating honestly with each other.

The Judge

When appropriate, you can use your authority and position to end conflict by enforcing a final resolution. Of course, you should have no stake in the outcome.

This role plays best when a conflict arises entirely within your department or work group. You can play the Judge outside your recognized area of authority, but only after you receive the acceptance of all parties involved.

The Judge's Tactics: Ensure a level playing field for all parties. Weigh the facts, arguments, and analyses. Then impose a resolution that is just, or at least one that leads to the best overall result.

RELATED TOPICS

Establishing Your Credibility, (pages 2–3)

Creative Problem Solving, (pages 98–99)

Empowering Your Employees

Inside Info

You empower your team by letting them assume responsibility for the details, while you focus your attention on larger issues of output and results.

Offer help, if needed, but instead of providing answers, provide only ideas and information on how the team can develop its *own* answers to the questions that come up.

There's a lot of talk today in supervisory and management circles about "empowerment." It's the idea that, instead of making employees dependent on specific instructions, supervisors and managers should give them the tools and flexibility to choose their own best ways to accomplish their work, and occasionally even what work to accomplish!

As team members assume increasing control over objectives, deadlines, and how best to meet them, they boost the organization's productivity by providing more of their best efforts, ideas, and loyalty.

But while it's easy to talk about empowerment, most people have no idea how to implement it. To help you, here are some ideas on how to empower the employees reporting to you:

Assign Bigger Projects

Next project:

It may take a little training and coaching, but good employees can learn to handle bigger projects as opposed to hour-to-hour or day-to-day assignments. You want them to develop the ability to determine what steps to follow, what sequence to put them in, and when to finish one and begin the next. When your people seem ready, you can try jointly developing, for example, an objective and deadline. Then you can let them pursue it independently.

Allow More Self-Scheduling

As you give employees larger assignments, give them commensurately more responsibility for scheduling what they do. With training, they can learn to finish the highest-priority tasks first, and then complete all of the project before it's due.

"I've got all kinds of time!"

At first, you might want to approve daily schedules drawn up by your employees. Later, as they develop confidence and skill in self-scheduling, you can move toward waiting to receive the completed work as it's finished.

Give Decisions to the Team

Experts say its best to push decisions down to the lowest possible level. For many projects, that's the front-line team of people actually doing the work.

You can build this kind of empowerment by deciding work-related matters in a cooperative way. For example, call a quick meeting. Describe the situation and the options you see. Ask your team members for their input, and then work to build a consensus. As this process becomes more familiar, team members will offer ideas, information, and creative solutions you never would have developed working alone. With this kind of team empowerment, decision making and implementation are generally far more successful than before.

RED ALERT! Watch for warning signs of "un-empowered" employees. Generally they:

- have little or no choice in decision making and work only on tasks the supervisor assigns them.
- offer little input and are nervous about deviating from established procedures.
- work alone, following established guidelines and making few if any decisions.
- are trained or qualified to do only a few tasks, day in, day out, with little grasp of the big picture into which they fit.
- feel less motivated and focus their interest on pay, vacation, and personal relationships.

RELATED TOPICS

➤ Valuing Your Employees, (pages 8–9)
➤ Giving Team Members More Effective Roles to Play, (pages 58–59)

Inside Info

The results of your decisions are the most important feedback you can receive to determine if you're decision-making skills are getting better—or worse.

Effective Decision Making

Decisions are no doubt easy for you. You've made thousands of them, and in many situations the best course to follow is probably quite obvious.

But to be more effective as a supervisor or manager, it's worthwhile to hone your decision-making skills in two ways: first, to make decisions easier and faster and, second, to make decisions that yield better results. By adhering to the following four steps, you'll be better equipped to make important, informed decisions:

1 Watch Effective Decision Makers

The best managers and supervisors in your organization surely possess excellent decision-making skills. Study what they do. Make it a habit to discuss their problems with them and ask about how they reached specific conclusions, decisions, and plans of action.

To facilitate your studies, keep a log of each decision you analyze—yours and those of the people around you.

DECISION

2 Log the Five Central Elements

For each entry in your decision-making log, note the following crucial factors:

- *Who makes the decision.* Knowing who's in charge will help you identify and learn from the best in the future.

- *Where he or she obtains needed information.* By tracking each decision-maker's favorite sources for facts, opinions, and ideas, you'll know where to go when researching your own upcoming choices.

- *Timing factors.* Some decisions are made on the spot, others over a period of days, weeks, even months. Knowing the chronology of successful decisions will help you learn when to push ahead rapidly, and when to let things stew a while longer.

- *The decision-making process.* This can involving solving a problem, choosing from many alternatives, or even selecting a strategic direction. Different processes work best based on each unique situation.

- *The quality of the results.* Decisions are only as good as the results they produce. So record how well each decision works out. This information helps keep your decision-making skills focused on the real world instead of the intellectual "ivory tower."

TimeSaver
If you find yourself in an uncomfortable decision-making process and you can delegate upward to your supervisor—who has more authority—do so.

RED ALERT! Don't get caught in the trap of overevaluating the minutia of a decision. Of course there are repercussions to every action—which you should be familiar with before making a decision—but not every decision is safe.

3 Correlate the Outcomes

Reviewing your decision-making log, you'll probably notice that some people make consistently better decisions than others, that individuals make better decisions in certain types of situations while groups make betters ones in others, and that some sources of information are unquestionably the most useful and accurate.

MAKING

4 Put Your Studies to Work

Keeping a log is a useful exercise, but the real test comes as you face tough decisions in the future. With practice, you should be able to spot:

- The main elements in the situation, and how they fit together.

- The times when a quick decision is appropriate, and when it isn't.

- The best decision-making method or process to use in any particular situation.

RELATED TOPICS

➤ **Effective Delegation,** (pages 10–11)

➤ **Managing Necessary Changes,** (pages 100–101)

If the extra time you've built into a project schedule turns out to be unnecessary, you can use it to do an even better job on some aspect of the project that would otherwise be short-changed or rushed.

Making and Meeting Deadlines

Deadlines can be one of the most effective supervisory and management tools in your arsenal. A well-chosen and steadily enforced deadline is a great way to help people prioritize, increase motivation and productivity, and eliminate downtime. A series of deadlines percolating throughout the organization can also improve overall coordination and cooperation.

But getting the most from deadlines requires two important supervisory and management disciplines: setting fair deadlines and then enforcing them.

To help you set deadlines that are fair and useful, here are some guidelines:

When Is It Needed?
Fair and useful deadlines reflect the dates and times when results are really needed, not necessarily the dates for which they're requested. For example, it's poor use of resources (and bad management) to demand that a report be finished today, but then let it sit unopened on your desk for a week. It's better to set each deadline by determining when—in the general flow of all the work now in process—you'll actually need to look at or use the results of this particular effort.

What Part Is Needed First?
Even when results are needed on a specific day, they may not all be needed at once. For example, say you're assembling 100 widgets and you need 100 prewidget subassemblies to do it. If you can make only 20 widgets a day, you really need only 20 prewidget subassemblies today, 20 more tomorrow, and so on. Similarly, you won't need more shipping boxes than you've got finished widgets to ship.

To help you guard against missing deadlines,
follow these techniques:

Schedule Backwards

Write down the steps needed to complete a project and the time
you'll need for each one. Then lay these out on a calendar,
starting with the completion date and working backwards.

   When you get to the starting point of the first step, you
know exactly when you must begin working on this project if
you want to meet its deadline.

D-Day

**Project
Due**

Day 7

**Phase
2**

Day 3

**Phase
1**

Day 1

**Begin
Project**

RED ALERT!

While priori-
tizing clearly
makes a dif-
ference, it's
not a good idea to finish
everything that's most
important and let it all sit—
ready for action—until it's
needed, while you then turn
to everything that's less
important, some of which
may have been needed a
few days ago.

   Instead, factor priority
and urgency together to
determine realistic dead-
lines for all of the tasks
you're trying to accomplish.

Allow Time for Unplanned Complications

Even if you can't be sure what will
go wrong, it's a safe bet that
midway through the project you'll
need extra time for some solid
reason. Include this contingency
time in your schedule now, and you
won't miss the deadline later.

"System error? What system error?"

RELATED TOPICS

➤ Avoiding "Reverse"
Delegation,
(pages 12–13)

➤ Creative Problem
Solving, (pages 98–99)

Inside Info

Make all your "visual management" charts neat, clean, and clear, with no erasures or spelling errors. But don't pay a professional to produce them. A "home-made" appearance can render these visuals less threatening to your team members and more user friendly.

Visual Management

It should be no surprise that most people understand and remember more of what they see than of what they hear. This is especially true for today's highly complex matters that can involve products and services that are intangible or difficult to grasp.

That's why more supervisors and managers are turning to visual aids as a way of providing frequent and vivid reminders of what their teams are supposed to be accomplishing.

Simply put, visual management is a concerted effort to use large-scale wall charts and other visual aids to keep your team more tightly focused on your messages, goals, and priorities. Here are the basics of how to supervise or manage more visually:

The Responsibility Matrix

	Answer Phones	Respond Inquiries	Enter Data	Customer Follow-up	Product Research	Market Research
Susan			★			
Jamal					★	?
Kyle		★				
Sanford	★					R
Jessica				★		

You can display even more information on this same chart without any further cluttering. For example, highlight the names of your assistants or lead workers to clearly identify them. Put a special symbol—like a question mark or a telephone—in the proper row and column intersection to show which of them is best qualified to provide other workers with help on specific topics. You can also vary the symbols in each person's row to show whether they're ahead of schedule, caught up, or behind.

On a chart set up like a chess- or checkerboard, put the names of the people you supervise or manage down one side, and the various projects or tasks to be done—such as answering phones, responding to inquiries, or entering computer data—across the top. Now you can convey a good deal of information just by putting something highly visible—a dot, a star, or just an "X"—at the intersections where the responsible person's row crosses the column containing the tasks he or she is supposed to be doing.

This kind of visual display helps each person recognize their own role within the team, as well as what the team as a whole is trying to accomplish. What's more, as responsibilities and tasks evolve over time, it's easy to update the chart to reflect the newer realities. Compared with trying to explain these concepts and responsibilities in words, this kind of matrix greatly reduces room for confusion and the tendency for certain tasks to remain ignored and undone for too long.

The Goal Board

Displaying individual and team goals more visually can jump start productivity by providing unmistakable guidance about where the team is headed and what tasks are most central to these objectives.

You can either display each goal on its own board or congregate them into a single visual. Select an icon or photograph that visually describes each important goal. Then list all the activities your team can pursue to help achieve it.

Catalog Mailing List Compilation	Acquire List	Cross-Reference	Deliver to Mail House
STATE			
Alabama	X	X	X
Arkansas	X	X	X
Arizona	X	X	
California	X		X
Colorado	X	X	
Delaware	X		

The Progress Tote Board

You've seen traditional fund-raising charts on TV telethons and elsewhere. They often look like thermometers or arrows pointing to a target.

Your own progress tote board probably won't have to change every day. But over weeks and months, you can update the chart to show how much closer your team is progressing toward a particular goal.

As it reflects this progress, the tote board provides a stimulating visualization to help team members understand how well they are actually performing.

GOAL

900,000
800,000
700,000
600,000
500,000
400,000
300,000
200,000
100,000

RED ALERT! It's easy to get caught up in the visual side of management and then neglect the "hands-on" side. Remember that, regardless of how many visuals you prepare for your department, they don't take the place of your supervision and guidance.

TimeSaver
Specialized software—such as certain project management and job tracking programs—can assist you and your employees with creating better visuals to work with.

RELATED TOPICS

➤ Setting Goals, (pages 26–27)

➤ Making and Meeting Deadlines, (pages 94–95)

Inside Info

Often there is more than one solution to a problem. If this is the case, evaluate your problem in the short and long term. What works today may not be appropriate in six months or a year.

Creative Problem Solving

When all is said and done, you earn your pay as a supervisor or manager with your ability to solve problems quickly and effectively. In fact, top managers generally acknowledge that improving their organizations' problem-solving capabilities is one of the best ways to increase their level of success.

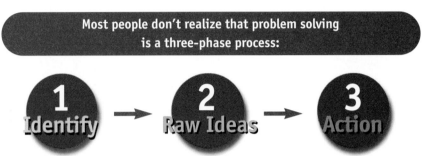

> Most people don't realize that problem solving is a three-phase process:

1 Identify → **2** Raw Ideas → **3** Action

First, identify the problem. Second, generate a lot of raw ideas about how to solve it. Third—and do this only after you've finished the first two—refine those raw ideas into practical, workable action plans.

The first step, of course, involves analyzing the situation to find discernible patterns that can lead you to the most likely cause of the problem you're trying to solve. Look for what happens immediately before the problem arises. What are the factors leading up to the problem? Who is involved with the problem? How do you know it *is* a problem?

Identifying the problem and its cause is usually the easiest part of the problem-solving process, like finding the leak in a plumbing system. Generally, the more clearly you can put your finger on what's wrong, and why, the easier time you'll have trying to fix it.

Once you've identified the problem, you're faced with the practical difficulties of how to solve it. This can be extremely frustrating, particularly when you're attempting to solve a problem within tight budget and other resource limitations.

> To help you with the problem-solving portion of your responsibilities, trying using one or more of these proven techniques:

Generate More and Better Ideas

• **Turn off your internal "critic"**
At this stage, it's important not to find fault and not to worry about practical implementation. Why? Because, for most of us, any hint of criticism or practical limitations dampens our creative

thinking process. The more wild and free-wheeling the ideas you and your team toss out on the table, the more useful raw material you'll have to work with later on.

• Forget the big picture
Focus individually on every element of the problem situation. Looking at how to change each one can give you dozens of raw ideas for possible solutions.

Idealize the World

Think in terms of "wouldn't it be great if. . ." Forget practical issues like technology, budget, human nature, and so forth, and focus instead on ideal changes you could make in a perfect world.

Convert Raw Ideas into Solutions

After you've compiled extensive lists of unedited and probably unworkable ideas, it's safe to begin processing them into practical possibilities for a realistic solution.

Begin with what appear to be the most promising ideas on your lists, and consider what changes you can make to convert them into something more workable and practical. When you can't do anything more with a raw idea, try to:

• Substitute or Combine
Put pieces of different ideas together to see if you can find a workable combination.

• Magnify or Minimize
Changing the sizes of things contained in your raw ideas can dramatically improve their practicality.

RED ALERT! Try not to force a solution to a difficult problem. In some cases, even when all the components are in place, there just isn't a simple answer. When this happens, temporarily put aside the issue and move on to other things. Then come back to it with a fresh mind and a bit more clarity on the situation.

RELATED TOPICS

➤ **Juggling Multiple Priorities, (pages 24–25)**

➤ **Motivation as a Daily Part of the Job, (pages 68–69)**

Managing Necessary Changes

Inside Info

Plan your introduction of changes at a pace that gives your people enough time to accept whatever adjustments and new ideas you're proposing. There's a natural resistance to any new idea or activity, but this resistance tends to dissipate as people become more accustomed to the new modification and see its advantages "up close." With a realistic timetable, you can introduce changes much more smoothly than with an overly ambitious one.

J ust about the only thing you can be sure of in today's workplace is that you can't be sure of anything! Working patterns, methods, technologies, tools, even terms of employment are changing so rapidly that those who lose their flexibility are likely to fall very far behind.

So supervisors and managers are now forced to add the role of "change agent" to their growing list of responsibilities.

To help you bring needed changes to your team and your workplace, here are some useful transitional techniques:

Change Issues

Don't blame those who are less willing to change. Look inside yourself. You'll probably see that you're unwilling to change too fast in certain areas. That's how most people generally operate. So don't condemn or criticize others who feel the same way.

Instead, focus your time and energy toward finding more effective methods of promoting the transitions that must take place. Think in terms of "motivation" rather than "pressure" and "commands."

WORDS TO LIVE BY

"The less things change, the more they remain the same."
—Sicilian proverb

Lead by Example...

rather than by command. You can try to win acceptance for important changes through informational meetings and the issuance of printed guidelines. But you'll get more people to follow the ideas and methods if you personally show your team how well the new techniques work for you.

To accomplish this, you'll have to overcome your own resistance to change before you try overcoming everyone else's. In some ways, it's more challenging to lead by example instead of by word—and it's generally more effective and fruitful.

Focus on Details

Put your energy into overcoming the specific objections, problems, and concerns your people bring you in response to the changes you propose.

This approach works well because, by attacking the substantive complaints and concerns that your people have, you pave the way for acceptance of the change you're trying to promote. If you eliminate their legitimate objectives, most of your employees will have an easier time accepting the new ideas.

Offer Emotional Support

Don't get angry at people's complaints about the new system. Instead, offer sympathy, understanding, and a willing ear. These complaints are signposts of their underlying emotional turmoil. By allowing your team to express these feelings—and by expressing some of your own —you facilitate a smoother acceptance of the changes to be implemented.

Tolerate Errors During Transition

One practical reason people tend to fear change is that they worry about how well they'll perform under the new system. That's why it's generally a very good idea to let your team know you'll be more forgiving of simple errors, mental oversights, and inadvertent reversions to the old ways of doing things during the first few days, weeks, or even months with the new system in place.

RELATED TOPICS

➤ Handling the Problems of Downsizing, (pages 60–61)

Glossary

Absenteeism—The rate at which individuals or entire work groups miss scheduled work days. Valid excuses make absenteeism less irresponsible, but excessive absenteeism is indicative of some type of problem.

Affirmative action—The set of laws, regulations, and company policies that seek to make a level playing field for groups of people who might otherwise have less chance for specific opportunities. Nothing in affirmative action recommends hiring people who are not qualified for a position.

Apprenticeship—A situation where a less-experienced employee is assigned to work with a more-experienced employee in order to learn the skills required for the job, and to augment the output of both employees. Apprenticeship is most effective when the assignments remain the same for a year at a time or longer.

Authoritarian—A leadership approach in which the boss is resistant to questions, suggestions, ideas, and particularly criticisms. In general, this approach has been proven to yield less satisfactory results than other, less rigid approaches.

Backstabber—A person who makes unkind or untrue comments about another and then tries to hide such behavior from as many people as possible.

Buddy—A person paired another for purposes of training and/or accomplishing daily work assignments.

Burnout—The sudden loss of enthusiasm, interest, and motivation for the job.

Cadre—A small group usually given special privileges and status.

Coaching—An approach to supervision that emphasizes the one-to-one relationship and replaces simply giving orders with a more interactive process where the "coach" takes the individual from his or her present level of competence and skill to a higher one. Coaching usually involves a low-pressure, interactive process.

Delegation—The process of getting others to accomplish parts of your responsibility by temporarily handing off to them enough authority, information, and contacts to perform the job. Delegation is also a good method to train those you supervise or manage.

Deliverable—A tangible work product expected to be passed from an individual to others, either within or outside the organization.

Empower—To give an individual or a team the freedom, flexibility, authority, and information needed to take more control of the workday, as well as to make and carry out decisions about what to do and when and how to do it.

Evaluation—The necessary process of determining how well, or how poorly, an individual is meeting his or her obligations and accomplishing his or her goals.

Flexible scheduling—A company policy that in various degrees allows employees to modify their working hours to meet family and community obligations that would normally interfere with work. Job sharing, flex-time, and other variable work options are forms of flexible scheduling.

Mentor—A person who shares his or her experience and knowledge with another, often to the mutual advantage of both. The best mentors are a combination coach, confidante, sounding board, and counselor.

Micromanage—The process of paying far too close attention to the details of what another person does, usually characterized by giving specific orders, suggestions, criticisms, and advisories.

Naysayers—People who habitually or by reason of personal characteristics always see the glass as "half empty," are reluctant to try anything new or depart from established procedure, and try to convince others that their negative view of life and work is both realistic and justified.

Perfectionism—An attitude embodying the idea that mistakes are a terrible problem and that any human error or departure from established standards is to be avoided at all costs. It often leads to spending more time and money than warranted on each task as well as an unwillingness to try new ideas or to take risks.

Priorities—The relative importance and urgency accorded to each of the many tasks, projects, assignments, and goals a person normally faces in a working situation. Priorities must be regularly reassessed so that the proper amount of time and energy is spent on each item on the agenda.

Probationary—Temporary and tentative. The early days, weeks, and months of employment are often implicitly or explicitly set up so that termination is easier and faster than it will become later on.

Punishment—A specific sanction imposed on an employee—ranging from an oral warning to days without pay to possible termination—applied as a response to unwanted behavior. Punishment should be appropriate and increased only gradually, but it often does less to change behavior than reward for what is desired.

Qualifications—The capabilities, experience, skills, and knowledge required to accomplish the responsibilities of a specific position. For various reasons, the stated qualifications for particular jobs frequently have little to do with the actual qualifications of those who are successful in that job.

Rebel—An employee who is less willing than most to follow all the rules without question. Too much rebelliousness can be difficult and dangerous, but sometimes a little rebellion helps a team find better ways to accomplish its work.

Self-management—The skill and ability to determine such matters as: which of several actions is the best to take in the immediate situation, what is the best response to a particular provocation, what resources are most needed for present and future success, and which of several opportunities is the best available.

Synch—Synchronization. Separate aspects of work that make sense and agree with each other are in synch. Those that don't make sense or that disagree with each other are out of synch.

Team spirit—The feeling that grows within a working group when one member can trust another and when the best interests of the group are felt to be aligned with the best interests of the individual.

Temp—A temporary employee. At one time, temps were hired strictly to replace long-term employees on vacation or sick leave. Today, temps often work for the same employer over long periods of time and may be "probationary" employees en route to being hired into permanent status.

Total compensation—The sum of raw wages plus other benefits, including paid vacation and sick leave, insurance, parking, telecommuting privileges, and many others.

Turnover—The rate at which established employees leave for other opportunities and must therefore be replaced. Turnover is extremely expensive, particularly when the now-vacant positions require people to have training and gain experience over a long time period.

Resources

Associations

American Society for Training and Development
1640 King Street, Alexandria, VA 22313. Phone (703) 683-8100

Books

The Corporate Coach: How to Build a Team of Loyal Customers. James B. Miller with Paul B. Brown. New York: St. Martin's Press, 1993.

The Deming Management Method. M. Walton. New York: Putnam, 1986.

Gendertraps—Confronting Confrontophobia, Toxic Bosses, and Other Landmines at Work. Judith Briles. New York: McGraw-Hill, 1995.

Learning to Lead: A Workbook on Becoming a Leader. Warren Bennis and Joan Goldsmith. Reading, Mass.: Addison-Wesley, 1994.

Managing People: 101 Proven Ideas for Making You and Your People More Productive from America's Smartest Small Companies. Sara P. Noble, ed. Boston: Inc. Publishing, 1992.

The New Manager's Survival Manual: All the Skills You Need for Success. Clay Carr. New York: John Wiley & Sons, 1995.

The New Woman Manager: 50 Fast and Savvy Solutions for Executive Excellence. Sharon Lamhut Willen. Lower Lake, Calif.: Asian Publishing, 1993.

Partnering with Employees: A Practical System for Building Empowered Relationships. Duke Nielsen. San Francisco: Jossey-Bass, Inc., Publishers, 1993.

The Seven Habits of Highly Effective People. Stephen R. Covey. New York: Simon & Schuster, 1989.

Successful Delegation: How to Grow Your People, Build Your Team, Free Up Your Time, and Increase Your Productivity. Frank F. Huppe. Hawthorne, N.J.: Career Press, 1994.

Talk It Out! 4 Steps to Managing People Problems in Your Organization. Dr. Daniel Dana. Amherst, Mass.: Human Resource Development Press, 1990.

13 Fatal Errors Managers Make and How You Can Avoid Them. W. Steven Brown. New York: Berkeley Books, 1985.

301 Great Management Ideas. Leslie Brokaw, ed. Boston: Inc. Publishing, 1995.

Magazines

Business Week (800) 635-1200

Entrepreneur—the Small Business Authority (800) 274-6229

Fortune (800) 621-8000

Inc.—the Magazine for Growing Companies (800) 234-0999 or (303) 604-1465

Sales and Marketing Management (800) 821-6897

On-line Services

America Online: (800) 827-6364, e-mail address: http://www.blue.aol.com/

Compuserve: (800) 848-8990, e-mail address: http://www.compuserve.com/

Prodigy: (914) 448-8000, e-mail address: http://www.prodigy.com/

Websites

Andersen Consulting: http://www.ac.com/
A site from a leading international management and technology consulting firm with 152 offices worldwide.

Deloitte & Touche: http://www.dttus.com/
Like having an on-line management consultant—includes library of over 400 separate entries linking to briefings, case studies, surveys, and other business issues. Deloitte & Touche is a 56,000-person organization with projects in 122 countries worldwide.

Galaxy Business Directory: http://www.galaxy.einet.net/galaxy/Business-and-Commerce.html
One of the most comprehensive business directories on the Web, with general categories like business administration, general resources, products and services, management, etc. Also includes business directories and glossaries, statistics, trends in international business, lists of general reading sources, libraries, periodicals, and information on business policy and legal issues.

Useful Organizations and Societies: http://www.ntu.ac.sg/~ctng/assoc.htm
One of the most comprehensive and up-to-date directories of major business, scientific, engineering, and educational societies on the web. Very high quality.

Yahoo Business Organizations: http://www.yahoo.com/Business_and_Economy/Organizations/
Best and most link-heavy directory of business organizations. Over twelve organizational categories including business development, consortia, foundations, professional organizations, and international trade, with brief descriptions at each listing.

Other Books in the Series

First Books for Business provide answers to your most pressing questions. In developing this series, we brought together an expert panel of top-notch businesspeople who shared their flair for success.

We know that the business world is chaotic and your time is valuable. So, we have taken the best of this panel's expertise and now present it in 50 colorful two-page chapters. Read it from cover to cover or use it as a reference guide. Either way, First Books for Business are your roadmap to business success.

Budgeting and Finance

To work effectively in today's marketplace, you must understand the importance of keeping projects "within budget." *Budgeting and Finance* demystifies the often confusing terms and paperwork associated with financial matters. This guide makes budgeting and finance principles easy to comprehend and will help you jump into the budget process with confidence. You'll learn how to:

- Determine your organization's budgetary needs
- Collect information to create a budget
- Interpret what budget and finance figures say about an organization
- Interact with others to develop a workable budget
- Read a financial statement

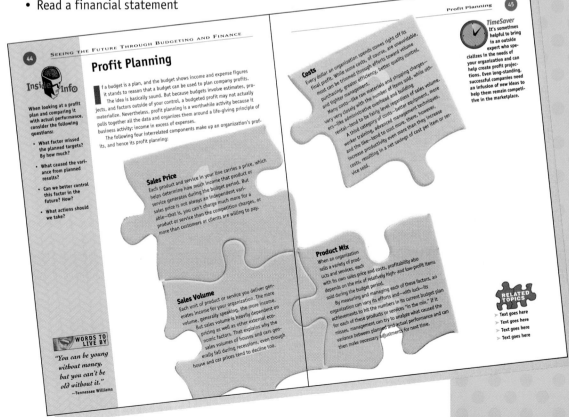

Business Presentations and Public Speaking

Knowing how to make a powerful presentation is the key to getting your point across in any business situation. *Business Presentations and Public Speaking* will show you how to increase the effectiveness of your presentation, whether in informal staff meetings or large conferences. You'll learn how to:

- Prepare an interesting, thorough presentation
- Capture your audience's attention
- Tell your audience what they want to know
- Sell them on yourself and your service or product
- Budget your time

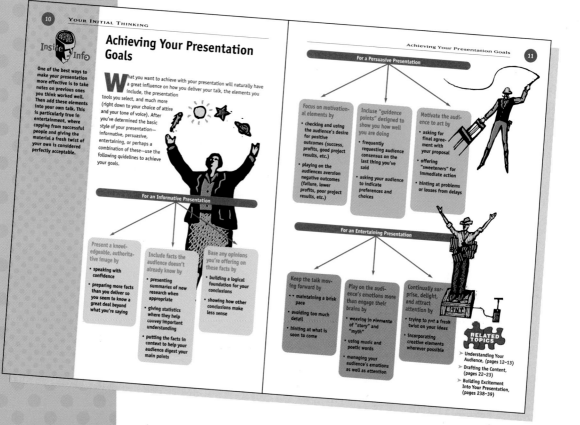

Negotiating

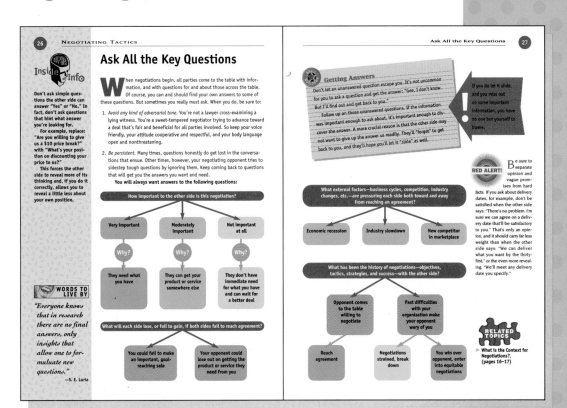

Understanding the art of negotiation is vital in your day-to-day-business dealings, whether you're negotiating a business contract with a supplier or a labor agreement with an employee. *Negotiating* teaches you how to negotiate strongly and effectively. This user-friendly guide will help you get exactly what you want, without your having to give up too much. You'll learn how to:

- Determine what you "want" versus what you "need"
- Structure the negotiations so both sides "win"
- Work with the personal dynamics of negotiating
- Get the most out of what you have to offer
- Turn around a losing trend

Sales and Marketing

Effective sales and marketing is key to the success of any business. *Sales and Marketing* sets forth the fundamental tools you need to effectively position your business. This user-friendly guide will show you how to create a marketing budget, perform research, and conduct marketing based on your organization's specific needs. You'll learn how to:

- Determine your marketing goals and objectives
- Identify and plan the strategy for reaching your markets
- Execute a tailor-made marketing campaign
- Evaluate the overall success of your efforts

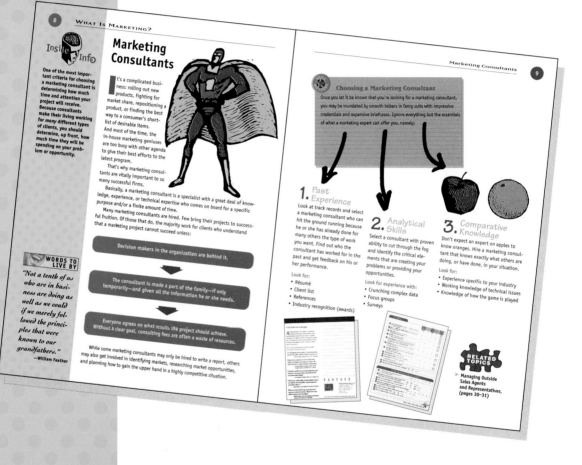

Index

Credits

Illustration

Art Parts: 9 bottom, 12, 13, 20, 21, 28, 29, 34, 35, 38, 39, 46, 47, 48, 49, 50, 51, 60, 67 bottom, 69, 76, 77, 78, 79, 80 bottom, 81, 82, 84, 85, 86, 90, 91, 94, 95 bottom, 98, 99, 100, 101; Frank Loose Design: 4-5, 6, 8, 9, 16, 25 top, 26 bottom, 33, 36 top, 52 top, 58 top, 63, 66, 67 top, 68, 80 top, 87, 95 top, 96, 97; Image Club Graphics, Inc.: 14, 15, 24, 25 bottom, 40, 41, 52 bottom, 53, 58 bottom, 59 62

Photography

Digital Wisdom, Inc.: 2, 30, 31, 36 center, 36 bottom, 42, 43, 44, 45, 54–55, 70, 71, 88, 89; Image Club Graphics, Inc.: 19; PhotoDisc, Inc.: 18, 22–23, 26 top, 27, 56–57, 65, 72, 73, 74